TODDLER DISCIPLINE

Peaceful Solutions and Strategies to Prevent
Conflicts Tantrums and to Raise a Happy Child

(Effective Strategies for Developing and Helping
Your Child)

Chad Barnes

Published By Oliver Leish

Chad Barnes

All Rights Reserved

Toddler Discipline: Peaceful Solutions and Strategies to Prevent Conflicts Tantrums and to Raise a Happy Child (Effective Strategies for Developing and Helping Your Child)

ISBN 978-1-77485-359-7

All rights reserved. No part of this guide may be reproduced in any form without permission in writing from the publisher except in the case of brief quotations embodied in critical articles or reviews.

Legal & Disclaimer

The information contained in this book is not designed to replace or take the place of any form of medicine or professional medical advice. The information in this book has been provided for educational and entertainment purposes only.

The information contained in this book has been compiled from sources deemed reliable, and it is accurate to the best of the Author's knowledge; however, the Author cannot guarantee its accuracy and validity and cannot be held liable for any errors or omissions. Changes are periodically made to this book. You must consult your doctor or get professional medical advice before using any of the suggested remedies, techniques, or information in this book.

Upon using the information contained in this book, you agree to hold harmless the Author from and against any damages, costs, and expenses, including any legal fees potentially resulting from the application of any of the information provided by this guide. This disclaimer applies to any damages or injury caused by the use and application, whether directly or indirectly, of any advice or information presented, whether for breach of contract, tort, negligence, personal injury, criminal intent, or under any other cause of action.

You agree to accept all risks of using the information presented inside this book. You need to consult a professional medical practitioner in order to ensure you are both able and healthy enough to participate in this program.

TABLE OF CONTENTS

INTRODUCTION 1

CHAPTER 1: DISCIPLINE 9

CHAPTER 2: POSITIVE PRAISE 22

CHAPTER 3: PARENTING TIPS TODDLER DISCIPLINE FUSSY EATERS 30

CHAPTER 4: HOW TO CORRECT BAD BEHAVIOR 36

CHAPTER 5: HELPING YOUR CHILD CONTROL THEIR EMOTION 40

CHAPTER 6: TAMING TANTRUMS 51

CHAPTER 7: TECHNIQUES TO DISCIPLINE YOUR TODDLER 71

CHAPTER 8: TODDLERS AND SIBLINGS 86

CHAPTER 9: CHILDREN'S DISCIPLINE TIPS FOR PARENTING' 97

CHAPTER 10: PHYSICAL AND MENTAL DEVELOPMENT .. 117

CHAPTER 11: THE FUNCTION OF COMMUNICATION 138

CHAPTER 12: COMBAT & BREATHING 150

CHAPTER 13: DIFFICULT TODDLERS 161

CHAPTER 14: DEALING WITH TROUBLESOME TODDLERS 173

CONCLUSION 181

Introduction

The process of disciplining a toddler isn't simple. It can be quite difficult since, in order to properly control your toddler requires an in-depth understanding of their mental development. Children between one and three does not have the capacity to think rationally as older children do. The mental maturity of this age doesn't permit him to grasp and remember all the rules you have set. Even if he is aware of how to apply the guidelines, he will not be able retain the rules for long. Beyond that the ability to empathize with other people, as well as the instinct to protect himself is still in the early stages of development. The understanding of logic as well as the ramifications of his actions are still in the early phases.

You should be aware that your toddler is in the early stages of developing their self-esteem, and will be eager to do all things for himself. He may want to take on things that he's not completely capable of at the moment. This can cause frustration or annoyance. This, in conjunction together with the reality that he's not entirely capable of communicating verbally, can lead to him venting his anger by throwing tantrums or engaging with inappropriate behaviors.

Another thing to be aware of when dealing with a child is that it may never be the intention of him to behave in a way that is inappropriate. Actually, the behavior he displays is his reaction to an event. He's responding to situations in the way that his lack of maturity permits him to. Therefore, you should be empathetic and understanding when you're working with your child. It is important to be aware of the various things your child is experiencing and his development. If you can be aware of these aspects it will be easier to react to the child's behavior when you have to discipline him.

Common Triggers

Before you begin to learn about methods and strategies that you can apply in teaching your children how to behave it is important to identify the triggers that are common. Most of the time, toddlers' misbehaviors usually occur as a result of the specific event or circumstance. What's the cause you're seeing him being disruptive? Parents are shocked when their child begins to display a rage and are extremely disappointed by this behaviour. Some parents even think that they are walking an emotional minefield surrounding the child, where anything could cause their child to become upset. It's certainly not something that is easy to handle parents often feel down and defeated as a result. However, you can reverse the situation and assist your child.

The root of the issue is not the situation, feeling or emotion. In reality, it's the child's response to these situations that is the issue. It is essential to recognize every issue that you want to fix or deal with the issue successfully. Begin by creating an outline of the factors that trigger the child on. When you have an inventory of all possible triggers, it is simpler to address the problems. The only way you can begin helping your child manage and control his behavior is to identify all triggers. The process of identifying triggers can be more easily managed when your child is able to communicate with you verbally. If you're working with a child who does not have the language skills needed to communicate the way he wants to, you'll have to be more sensitive with the child.

In determining the triggers that cause him to be upset, you are equipping yourself with the information you need to devise efficient methods to help him control his mood. Additionally it also gives you an understanding of the scenarios you should be aware of.

Your child may be prone to throwing temper tantrums when he is hungry, tired or is suffering from physical discomfort. As he does not have the ability to convey what he's feeling, throwing a rage outrage is the most effective way to declare "Enough!" He's trying to convey your feelings in the only manner that he can think of is by screaming, flailing around and whining or through kicking and screaming.

As a toddler isn't able to communicate how he feels and is often dissatisfied with his capabilities. There may be a myriad of things he would like doing, but he's or isn't strong enough to perform these things or lacks the necessary coordination to do the similar task. It could be that is as easy as creating a toy. This, along with the inability of him to express his feelings, increases his frustration verbally. Disruptive behavior, displays of acquisitiveness, or angry outbursts are his only ways he is able to let out the anger that he is feeling. Be aware that your toddler is at a point in which he is unable to exercise any control over his anger.

Adults struggle with controlling their urges and desires. This is why it's not surprising that toddlers are more likely to have the same issues. If an adult of all emotional maturity can't manage his emotions so how can you expect a child to manage his needs or urges? He not only has difficulty demonstrating the control he requires and he is also assuming that all of his desires will be fulfilled. Therefore, if one of his demands is refused, or his desires are not met The toddler is bound to be dissatisfied. Children often have a difficult dealing with their emotions when they hear "no." Additionally they are also struggling with comprehending the reasons the reason their demands weren't fulfilled. The concept of delayed gratification is not appear in the vocabulary of a toddler.

A toddler isn't able to comprehend much or has any understanding of the world that surrounds him. The majority of the behavior that is displayed in him is due to his interest. Remember that your child is seeking to understand his surroundings, and the way things function and how they live. In doing so you may see him suggest that he is crossing the line of what is thought acceptable behavior. For example, he could be able to pull the dog's tail since it is his desire to observe how it reacts. He could also throw the spoon around the room to observe the sound it makes. All of these could be an issue for parents, but as a child's viewpoint These are actions that help keep him interested.

As your child begins to grow, he'll be aware of his own ability. When he is aware of the power he has, he will keep testing the limits of the things you can let him do. It's not a bid to cause trouble However, he's trying to understand the depth of his ability.

Every child loves attention. A toddler's love of attention is unique to any other. Unwanted attention is something that your toddler can't take. No matter if the focus he receives is positive or not, he wants it. The majority of the inappropriate behaviours that toddlers display is their demand for attention. They love being surrounded by continuous attention. If this attention is slowed due to reasons beyond their control they will engage in behaviors that shift attention to them.

Another reason that can cause your toddler's bad behavior could be any major changes. One example of a significant change in a child's life could be the introduction of an additional babysitter, while an insignificant change could be the reduction in play time. If such changes happen they are likely to make your toddler feel overwhelmed emotionally. Since he's unable to articulate how is bothering him, he may turn to venting his anger out through screaming.

Chapter 1: Discipline

There is no doubt that you'd love to have a calm, well-behaved kid. There's a chance that you're being pressured by family members, friends and even strangers you meet in the street to make sure that your little one is polite and calm. The good news is you can have a child who behaves. The bad newsis that you cannot have one all the time. Because of the nature of the human brain's development, children need patience, time and direction to understand how to behave with respect towards others and control their own emotional state.

What is discipline?

How can you get children behave? It could be surprising You don't. The child is the only one who can alter his behavior within the limits of his developmental abilities. However, you hold the power to influence his behavior as his caregiver. You can assist him in making the decision to obey or comply with your demands as well as help him understand the behavior requirements for various situations in your family culture. He needs discipline. To employ the transitive verb to emphasize the point you need to make sure he is controlled by your presence.

Parents and experts continue to debate the best way to discipline young children should look like and there are numerous strategies you could try. Punishment is likely to come to the mind, but routinely punishments like smacking or spanking, isolation or removing items, privileges, or even experiences from children may have unintended consequences later in the course of. If you are using punishment as a method of discipline you're sending children the impression that you do not want to be punished for the actions he has committed. In his unconscious it is creating the impression that your affection is equivalent to your approval.

Many adults who suffered severe punishment as children experience high levels of stress which can cause anxiety, guilt, or depression. Many struggle to maintain healthy, trustworthy relationships with other people. Contrary to this, the rational recourse to consequences that may include removing your child from a risky or problematic area, does make the same effect. The setting of limits for unacceptable or unsafe behavior can lead to positive outcomes

Quick Tip: It may be difficult emotionally to be able to disapprove of the way that our parents have raised us. Disagreeing with the discipline method doesn't diminish the value of a friendship or diminish the positive contribution of an individual. Because your parenting journey requires an amount of reflection I suggest that you admit any feelings that are uncomfortable and remain open while you study the tips offered here.

In search of positive alternatives to punishment, parents frequently opt for praise and rewards to promote good behaviour. The advocates of this method suggest giving out treats, stickers or other treats to encourage the compliance. If the promise of your approval isn't more enticing enough to deter the risk of breaking the rules the children could decide one day to accept the reward. It's not an issue if the offence is small for instance, when a teenager isn't willing to shut off the television before bedtime. It's a huge problem when the breaking of the rules harms the person in question, other people or the surroundings, such as driving drunk.

A better way of discipling the child you love is to employ techniques that allow him to discern moral judgements regarding right and wrong for him. That doesn't mean that you let him choose what he'd like to do. As just a toddler, you're the only person who can make any important decisions that you think are best for him. Because a toddler isn't equipped with the capacity to use reasoning or logic to resolve problems or determine the appropriate behavior in any circumstance, you are teaching him step-by step. The child's independence will be gaining momentum by making easy, sensible decisions at first. If he lets go of his huge emotions and loses controlof his emotions, you'll offer your assistance by empathizing with him and giving him the boundaries he requires to feel secure and appreciated.

Set realistic goals

Parents frequently have expectations of behaviors that aren't realistic for the children's ages. Short-term goals

There will come a time where you have to establish an amount and then decide whether to enforce the limit quickly or let it go of your preferred routine. Here are some examples of common short-term goals that relate to issues with behavior.

Conformity for the sake safety:

A good night's rest:

Using good manners:

Stopping the whining

Long-Term Goals

Spend a few minutes to create your own list. Start by thinking about what you believe as your strengths as well as your experiences that helped build your strengths. Think about the values of your family and community. What do you think is an important value?

If you decide to pick from the various methods of discipline you are considering, be sure to consider whether they are in line with the long-term goals that you've determined are important to the future of your child. For instance, if you give your toddler an easy choice of wearing a red or a blue one it's a simple positive act of discipline that will not only help to avoid a meltdown in the morning and builds autonomy and responsibility. If you sit down with your four-year-old and have a meaningful discussion about why not excluding someone from a group activity can be harmful, you're instilling compassion.

The process of disciplining your sometimes erratic hyper-emotional toddler can be difficult. To keep in mind these goals for the future You could even save your list at a spot in which you'll see it frequently, like on your fridge or in your purse or on the door of the front.

Temperament and Behaviour

Your style of parenting will be a major influence on the way your child behaves and sees his position in the world, however, it's not the sole aspect to consider. A majority of people think that the character of a child is always the result of how permissive, or even dictatorial your parent. It's a myth. Your child is an individual and valuable human being who was being born predisposed towards certain traits that were developed in the uterus and continued to develop through the experiences she had throughout her early years.

In a groundbreaking study of infants' reactions to stimuli Alexander Thomas, Stella Chess as well as Herbert G. Birch determined that the child's "personality is developed through the constant interaction of temperament and the environment." These nine traits of temperament identified in this study offer an understanding of why children who are raised in similar environments can differ from one another.

The level of physical activity attribute is a measure of your child's overall level of energy. A child with a high energy level can be quite a nuisance due to all their squirming, wiggling and screaming as a sedentary child is difficult to get motivated physically, since peaceful, quiet activities are the most sought-after. If your child is always climbing up furniture, bouncing in circles, and slipping into and out of bed in the late at night, make sure that you allow her outdoor access on a regular basis so that the muscles can freely move. Inside, look for ways to meet the need for stretching and explore on her own.

Rhythmicity: How reliable is your child's normal biological rhythm? Some children take a nap, eat and have frequent bowel movements. For them, a regular routine is comfortable and is largely dependent on themselves. Others children exhibit much more fluctuation, which could cause problems with naps, meals and toilet training. Intervention by parents and flexibility are essential to prevent conflict.

Distractibility: Does your child seem easily distracted by the outside world? Children with high levels of distraction is usually content when you swap an unsafe object with a secure toy, or sing a tune while doing something uninteresting like buckling in a vehicle seat, or changing diapers. Children who are less inclined to get disoriented will continue to be distracted until the task is completed.

First reaction: When faced by a brand new circumstance like a stranger, food item item, activity, or toy How eagerly is your child embracing the experience? Some kids approach them easily, quickly engaging and interacting impulsively. Some are slower to warm up, and take time to settle in and evaluate the situation. If children are introduced someone new for example, a babysitter, she could prefer sitting on your lap and observe for a few minutes before engaging. However, the eviction of children from new situations is more dramatic and requires a lot of parental support and patience. Children who have an initial negative reaction to new circumstances may run away, cry or even run away. They will require emotional support and plenty of time to adapt to new situations.

Adaptability: This is the ability of your child to adapt as time passes to new experiences routines, routines or even expectations. If your child is able to adapt in their personality, the transition from one activity to the next is not a huge problem. The transition to a new routine might take some time, however, you shouldn't be met with objections from your kid. Some children may react negatively to new routines such as through outbursts, defiance or anxiety-related behaviors. They will be able to appreciate gradual changes in routine , not dramatic ones.

Attention span and perseverance Do your children focus on one thing for an extended period of duration? Do they keep going back to the same task and learn new skills in spite of any obstacles? The child who has higher levels of focus and perseverance does not quit easily when asked to complete tasks that may initially be difficult. However when you interrupt the same child to request for her to switch to a different task You may be confronted with resistance and a rigid attitude. If your child has a smaller focus and less perseverance is she likely requires a more systematic approach, reminders and visual cues to assist her in completing difficult tasks.

Intensity of reactions How intensely does your child express his emotions? Children who are extremely emotional may be labelled "overdramatic," celebrating with excitement to the extreme and screaming or crying about minor disappointments. Children with less intenseness may cry or smile however in general, their reactions to events are much more restrained when compared to other children.

Sensory threshold: When exposed to a variety of physical sensations, will your child react positively either negatively or positively or at all? Certain children are highly sensitive to sensory stimuli like noise or light which can make the crowded and noisy environments challenging to maneuver. Some will respond differently and seek out additional stimulation for the sake of it.

Qualities of mood What is your child's mood? Does he generally appear happy and optimistic or display an untrustworthy and serious attitude? The mood of your child's can naturally vary from day to day however, in general, children are inclined to a more positive state of mind or less positive one.

Human personalities are unique however, they are all beautiful and complement each other. Anywhere one's child's personality falls within the spectrum of of these characteristics, she should be respected and appreciated for the person she is and what she will become. Certain situations will be more manageable for her to handle and certain methods of discipline are better than other strategies. If you know how she reacts to life's events and challenges, you'll be able to understand her struggles, select one of the best parenting strategies and help her transition into the adulthood stage.

Chapter 2: Positive Praise

Let me you know to answer this...

If you're at work and your boss walks in and looks over the stack of papers you've already processed and gives you a high-five What does it feel like? It's good, isn't it? It encourages you to do more. It's nice knowing that someone appreciates the work you're doing. It's satisfying to know that someone has recognized the good work you've done.

So, I have some something to share with you. It's a strategy to encourage you to be more productive. Sure, they noticed the fact that you're doing more than other employees otherwise they wouldn't have been able to see your effort however, they don't have to congratulate your efforts. The work you're doing is part of the job description. It's the standard for you to follow. When you're being praised, it makes everything more enjoyable. This gives you something to boast to your colleagues about, or even to your spouse.

Human beings want the love of others, regardless of how much we try to convince ourselves the opposite. We love it, and we want to take in all the wonderful things that are said towards us. We want to be surrounded by the praises and praises. It's no surprise that this is widely used to encourage employees to carry greater than they can handle. When it is effective, it's effective. Why not apply the same approach with your child?

Praising Your Toddler

Toddlers are awestruck by praise and enjoy being told that they're doing a good job. Young children have more senses when it comes to these issues than adults do. The burdens of life haven't removed their natural abilities yet.

As I've said before it's normal for people to want the acceptance of their peers. Your child looks up to you and will be looking at you throughout all of lives. The moment they get your approval, it's something they are very proud of. If they know they'll be rewarded when they're good, then why should they do anything wrong? The majority of children, but not all, are prone to misbehavior because they don't receive enough praise. They are prone to misbehave in order to gain your notice. This is the only method they have to use.

When you praise your child in your speech, you are telling your child what you want them do and what you would not approve of the way they behave. This gives them the motivation to behave, since they're being noticed by you even and they're not being good What is the reason they would wish to be a bad person?

Praise is also a wonderful method of building confidence in your child's self from the beginning and encourage them to be positive about themselves and the actions they take. It teaches your child that the things they're doing are right and they deserve the praise they're receiving.

If a child keeps being disciplined, there's a great likelihood that they'll question all they do to the next time around. They will not strive to achieve great things because the only thing they've ever receive is a scolding and disapproval regardless. So, the majority of kids behave out.

We express disapproval without being aware of that we are doing it. Simple things such as "you have put your toys into the wrong boxes" could make your child think that they'll ever be able to act in a responsible manner. In their minds the act is viewed with disapproval, and they will not repeat it. They don't realize it's not the right box. They simply know it's just a box. Replace the phrase with "thank you for putting all your toys away. You're so adept at this, why not put it in that box again next time." The idea is to help your toddler realize the message that "wow mommy/daddy is happy" and will do to ensure that it stays that way.

Praise can be used to accomplish various things, such as placing toys away, or even taking down the doll as it's time to get dressed. It can be a bit tedious at times however, it is effective. Your child will know exactly the time to praise them and the best way to earn it. They're smart.

Making Choices

It's weird to give children the option of choosing does it? In reality, this creates a sense authority and control. Similar to grown-ups and children they want to have an input into the activities they do. They will learn to make wise decisions and face the consequences of poor choices. Certain children aren't concerned about having choices , and will accept whatever you instruct they should do. Some children will lashing out and be angry.

If you make decisions for them, you influence who they will be currently on the path to becoming. The individual must make decisions that will determine them in a particular direction. Despite the opinions of many parents that their choices aren't always the most beneficial for their children. In addition, the consequences on them as they get older. Indecisiveness is often due to an inability to make the choices that children make as they grow up. When you're not forced to choose what will you do when you are required to make a decision? This will make you doubt your own abilities and the choice you're going to make.

Ich am among them. I'm not able to save my life but that's not because of a inability to do so by my parents. They pushed me at a very young age to take decisions. Certain people are wired differently. It is a parent's duty to do everything that they can to promote the capacity of their child in making their own choices regardless of whether someday they'll encounter indecisiveness. This can also assist you with parenting. Nobody wants to be the parent of an infant until they're married and so the idea of teaching children from an early age to make wise choices will allow you to avoid these situations in the greatest extent possible.

The best thing to consider is to settle on simple choices that don't be too disruptive like asking your child what stories they'd prefer to hear or if they'd want for them to have a playdate with dolls or make craft projects today.

It is important to provide your toddler with choices, so that you are able to agree with every choice they take. When you inquire if they'd like to participate in crafts however expect to be pleasantly surprised when your child has an outright screaming fit. Instead, substitute crafts with something they can complete on their own in the event that you're not able to supervise them. Avoid asking questions such as "do you wish to rest?" because the answer is likely to be "no" majority of the times. If you ask your child to nap it will make them feel as though they were forced to take a nap the time you asked them and they'll be hesitant to make decisions in the future.

It's a wonderful method of teaching your child how to behave. If your child is getting angry and making choices, remove them. Inform them of the reason for their behavior and why you're taking this action. This is a great way to punish any child. Make sure to praise your child whenever they are making choices!

Controlling Release

It is not easy for any parent to think through. It is important to recognize that there are some things that you can't manage. In addition, there are things that could go in different ways than the ones you choose to follow.

If you're keeping the leash tight on your child, it's common for them to get into trouble and feel stuck. When you allow your child to make an option, you're not only giving up some sort of control, however you're making your life more manageable. Children behave better when they feel they have a choice the situation.

Nobody likes being managed, and some toddlers display the signs of this from a young age. It is better to let go of this tiny bit of control rather than struggle with a child who is unruly for the rest of their lives.

Chapter 3: Parenting Tips Toddler Discipline Fussy Eaters

Your child could be a cautious eater, and a snare to experiment with a new food. The majority, or less than half of all toddlers have this mindset and it's not surprising that food-related issues are the cause of anxiety for parents. The process of setting the scene...
7
How can you teach a toddler independence
Two-year-old children generally attempt to demonstrate their confidence in themselves. Sometimes, it can be hilarious, when archetype back when a toddler has to put on clothes and he may occasionally make parents mad when their child is determined and doesn't want to eat and throws food all over the kitchen. Parents can also feel helpless because their infant doesn't wish to be accepted by their child. What can you tell the toddler's

abilities after they go insane? 2 years old children generally attempt to prove their self-confidence. Sometimes it could be hilarious, for example, if archetype when a toddler has dressing himself, however, it could also make parents insane when their child is stubborn and isn't hungry and scatters the food everywhere in the kitchen. Parents might also be frustrated because their infant doesn't have the desire to be accepted by their child. What can you do to help the toddler's abilities after going insane? First of all parents must think that it's a valid assurance when their child is trying to be self-sufficient. This means that their child develops well and is curious. They also have confidence in that it is strong, has the support of his parents, however, he also wants to show as big and capable of doing things independently. own.However the baby-like adolescent does not yet understand that there are limitations and guidelines, that certain things are not allowed and have to be completed in a certain way and additional things must be accomplished more than what a baby can do. There are misunderstandings that are sometimes amusing, but can also be frustrating for parents. Here are some ideas on to help your child abut his accustomed to aggression and help him develop his independence.Parents must be patient and establish some guidelines that can be altered, in line depending on the new abilities of the child. For instance, at beginning, the child can be able to access and attaching to the Velcro in his shoe, place an abbreviate or cap, and mother is the one who closes the zipper on his jacket.Before you start dressing your child (and change the subject of what he can abrasion today) You should make the following: He can put his socks on his feet, however you will guide him with sneakers. Because of this, the adolescent feels that he also is superior over the bathrobes and understand the importance of his duties.Parents may also let their child choose the outfit he prefers but don't let him take two options and not all the clothes that are in the closet! Let the child decide whether you want to wear abrasion-dejected or amber pants or if the sweater he chooses is for dogs or a car.Remember that adolescents do grow more slowly and does not feel the need to rush. Therefore, if you're planning to allow your child to take a stroll and walk, it is important to increase the alertness before hand to give your child plenty of time. Because of this, you don't have to worry that you'll be stumbling backwards. In addition, you could have fun and if your child is a teenager, that bathrobe could be fun.If your child is causing you stress to display his independence, you could utilize it when teaching the rules of hygiene to him. To make it more adorable for your baby you could purchase soap with the look of his favorite beast or a soap with vibrant images on the packaging. You could also allow your child take his most loved toy into the tub for ablution (of the latest technology, ensure that the toy can be used in an play in water). Additionally, you can purchase an hydrator that is bright and adorned with your child's favourite car, animal or even a character from the movie.Parents must allow their children to eat their meals on their own, just as when they eat with their hands! Similar to babies of a few months, they are able to eat on their own. After a while , you could offer your child an ice cream cone or an angle that is made of advanced artificial varieties that are appropriate for infants. It is also possible to allow your child to choose what food he likes just give him two choices and not 10! This way, your child will be able to develop his own dietary preferences and adapt his bistro habits. Additionally, bistro-apart is also a frequent affliction to the allocation of convenances and movement precision.The teenager wants to emulate the behavior of his parents, but the fact that he's a baby can be a problem. You should be aware of your surroundings and contemplate ways to assist him in his routine tasks as well as make the usual tasks with less effort. Install a sturdy footfall stool to allow him to change his position to turn the flame to turn it off and on. The footfall stool for adolescents is also useful in bathing - it will be abutting the toilet, sink, and tub. It is also possible to use it in the kitchen so that your adolescent can help on how to modify your meals. Set up a hanger for your the anorak of your child so that he can have the ability to wear it.Before you allow your child to complete circadian tasks independently (like dressing, abrasion tooth bathing or eating) establish the guidelines for what the child does independently and how you will help him.For instance, teaching your child to besom his teeth every day could be a great way to show appreciation to parents' patience. Adolescents can beef up and even sand in order in order to deny his teeth. There are a few ways to deal with this scenario. The baby's mom can besom her teeth, and babyish may besom the mother's teeth. It is also possible to tell an story about a crocodile who scrubs bird's teeth, and makes hilarious smiles. Songs for teenagers that are funny can available in abrasion classes.

Chapter 4: How to Correct Bad behavior

In the context of parenting, bad behaviors should not be tolerated regardless of the cause. The aim is to offer an alternative that is healthier or a proper means of expression. What toddlers do not have yet, and they require instruction on how to practice what is considered acceptable behavior.

Provide Consequences

To stop bad behavior, you can choose one of two approaches or both.

Different Effects

If your toddler isn't paying attention or has been ignoring your demands more than three times in a row even though they've been given a few choices, it's now possible to make use of the concept of consequences.

If, for instance, your child is constantly grabbing toys from another child even though they've been set just a few feet away, and being warned, you can impose the appropriate consequence, like taking away his own toys or even removing him from the play area entirely.

The results are, as you can observe, differ based on the circumstances and are usually carried out with a proper warning.

Timeout Method

This Timeout method is essentially similar, however it is based on being placed in one location for the duration of time until your child can be permitted to return. If your child is a troublemaker even after being warned, set him in the end of the room, away from other children. The idea is to keep the child from other children or to determine which is where "fun" is, and when he decides to return there the child must be taught to behave.

The Timeout method may not always work as its effectiveness is dependent on the way it is implemented and the child's personality. Timeouts should not be utilized for toddlers who aren't yet. Children aged between 4 and five years old are better able of comprehending the implications of a timeout than children older children, specifically those between 2 and 3 years old. older.

Consistency

Perhaps the most difficult aspect of parenting with positive discipline generally is the being consistent. As parents, you'll require every bit of patience and understanding you discover in yourself. It is also necessary to show the same level of understanding and patience each and every day.

The lessons you impart today, you'll teach the following day, and each day throughout your children's lives. Being a parent isn't easy as you're a parent all the time and you'll be instructing your child on good behavior, leading by instance, as well as correcting poor behaviour. This is all you'll be doing until your child is able to learn to speak for themselves.

Your consistent behavior will form the foundation of your child's discipline. If, regardless of the situation is or what your child does, you never compromise or change your rules, he'll expect nothing less and become more observant. Modifying the method that you manage your children regularly isn't just complicated, it could become the reason he doesn't be able to listen to you anymore.

Encourage Good Conduct

A key part of positive discipline is paying attention to the positive behavior of your child. The most common thing parents don't do is take note of or pay attention to the good choices their child is already displaying. Many parents believe that just correcting bad behavior will cause only good behavior. However, actually, you should be a positive influence to ensure that bad behavior does not come back.

Chapter 5: Helping Your Child Control Their Emotion

Many parents want to see their children manage with their emotions without breaking down or blaming their frustrations onto others. It's hard to watch your children react to their feelings of anger with rage, anger, the blame, blaming or even obstructing people surrounding them when their emotions are at a high. As parents, we face moments when we aren't aware of what to do.

Let's face it; it isn't easy for every person to manage our emotions. We all can lose it every now and then or let our emotions appear to improve our own. Furthermore, a couple of kids deal with their complicated feelings--feelings of disillusionment, dread, outrage, hurt or frustration--extremely well. The distinction between kids with adults, is adults have figured out how to deal with these emotions effectively, whereas youngsters haven't quite mastered the art of it yet.

What Does This Look Like

What is that like? There are temper tantrums. They cry, pout, and lash out at others and break things, panic or take their anger out on other people, avoid the person in front of them, don't participate in a whine, complain, keep a grudge and spew negativity. They don't only act out, they can also "act in" like James Lehman said, by giving them the silent treatment, and ignoring you passively. I refer to this as "spilling the black color" throughout the home.

Why is it so difficult for kids to learn control their emotional state? It's much easier for all of us to allow others to take responsibility and to pick up the pieces. If you do not have to confront the emotions that come with it, then it's more easy to not do it, especially in the event that someone else is doing the job for us. Sometimes, children are led to believe that they aren't able to handle emotional turmoil on their own and require help from assistance from others to work through their emotions.

It's normal for children their strong reactions to trigger your feelings of anxiety, anger and uncertainty. This can cause you to become angry, too. The eruptions of children can be quite a shock and leave us confused about how we can help. Of course, after the years of trying to soothe them when they were children We rush into them from routine. (And throughout the years you've probably discovered that any attempt to comfort or assist even with the best intentions, may be a disaster and cause them to be upset more.)

What's the trigger for your child?

Each of us has particular areas of vulnerability that are particularly sensitive to us. For certain, it's about disdain, for others , it could be related to acceptance, inequity pride, autonomy, or injustice. These areas of vulnerability are often referred by the name of our "triggers," because when one of them is pulled, it triggers an immediate reaction within us.

When someone presses one of our buttons without intention, we typically get angry or frustrated with that person.

I know a young man named Eli* who gets it each time a teacher, parent or a friend gives him instructions. Eli is a strong and sensitive sensitivity to his own independence. This is one of his triggers and an element that can cause him to be angry and to engage in a fight with his peers.

What Eli does not realize the reality is, if Eli didn't hold the button, it wouldn't be pushed in any way in any way. If he weren't as affected by the notion that is "independence," for example and the sensitivity to being directed to do something then he wouldn't get angry frequently.

Unaware of this trigger makes him vulnerable, and allows others to have the ability to make him feel depressed or angry. He doesn't realize that the advice given to him on what to do is a reaction of his own and that he's reacting to something in him. He keeps blaming others and attempting to convince them to stop, instead of accepting the on the responsibility for his own trigger.

Eli is not the only one. We all have a myriad of factors that we're not aware of. We are constantly angered at people who deliberately or unintentionally press our buttons, without realizing the fact that we gave them an item to press.

Here are a few other instances. 13-year-old Sidney would scream in anger when she believed that her sisters or friends were "acting as if they were more than she were." Her sensitivity was mostly centered around her feelings of pride. 10 year old Jake is upset when any one criticizes him. His parents claim it's like walking on eggshells in order to be around Jake. The triggers for him were related to concerns of approbation.

What do I do?

Parents can be supportive of their children by helping them develop self-awareness. For instance, you could tell the child "I observe that often you become triggered when you feel that something isn't fair.

Are you aware of this?" Or, "I find you frequently angry when people argue with you, like you're not being valued. This is a good trigger for your." Of the course, giving your child feedback could cause them to feel angry, especially if they're especially sensitive about the way you view their behavior, so make sure you know this when you enter. (If this is the case, request your spouse or another trusted adult to hold this discussion with them.)

Be aware that you'll be more useful for your kids if you focus to increase your self-awareness. Take note of your triggers and try to eliminate them. This will assist you in learning to control your emotions and allow you to be less receptive to your child's sensitivities, which could be one in the same. (The benefit? If you do this, everyone will be more calm in the process.)

Deactivating the Buttons

How do sensitivities get rooted? That is what is the process by which the buttons come into being in the beginning? Where did they originate and how do we learn to better respond to them and encourage our children to achieve the same?

Triggers are based upon our brains, and are often influenced during the first years of childhood through the way in which our parents and family members behaved and reacted to us. While the situations may have changed and they are not as relevant however, we can still react in a way that makes sense to us today, and so even the smallest of things could "set our minds off." This is applicable to your child.

1. You can ask yourself these questions:

What are the most common circumstances that trigger your child's alarm? What is it that triggers your alarm?

What are the buttons? What do you have? (Are they identical?)

What categories would you place the majority of your buttons? What would you describe your child's?

Here are a few typical examples:

Approval
Pride
Injustice

Autonomy

Respect

Envy

Shame

Once you've identified the child's triggers, talk to him about what you've observed. Ask your child "How will you behave differently the next time? When you next think you're not fair What can you do to respond in a manner that isn't kicking the wall, screaming and cursing or breaking the object?" Have your child brainstorm ways to handle the situation. Think about asking him to create some ideas of what that he could do when he's upset.

2. Believe that the child is able to manage herself. It is important to believe that your child is able to handle her emotional needs by herself. Parents often rush in and attempt to "fix" problems. It's true that seeing your child's emotions get extremely difficult and cause us to feel overwhelmed and helpless. If you do step in and try to fix the child's issues for her be aware that you're perpetuating the problem. If you are too sympathetic in order to help the

child's feelings better you could add overly much "weight" onto the issue and increase the severity of it. The child will then get the impression that it's worse than she believed and only dad or mom will help her fix it.

The bottom line is Do not get involved in your child's emotional turmoil due to guilt or because you want to help your child feel more comfortable. Instead, consider "She's experiencing an uncomfortable feeling that she must deal with. I'm standing next to her box, but I don't need to get involved."

There is no need to assist your child navigate difficult emotions by analyzing every emotion together. It is possible to be compassionate but without saying "Oh you poor child!" If you react and pay attention to each emotion or mood your child is experiencing it will be what she will learn and accept. Better to say "I understand it's difficult, and you're frustrated and angry. You should take some time for your own feelings. Once you're done, meet us for a drink."

3. Do not minimize or cause your child to feel that his feelings do not matter "wrong". On the other side on the spectrum there are parents struggle with dealing with their child's feelings. As a result, they may attempt to convince their child that they're not feeling right by saying, "Why are you crying over this? It's ridiculous!" or "You're angry over that?" Give them the respect and the space to deal with their emotions by themselves regardless of whether it appears ridiculous or like they're reacting too much. (This isn't a reason for them to be rude or behave with others in the family in a rude manner. This is just a way to ensure they'll be allowed to process their feelings by themselves in their bedroom for instance.)

4. First, calm yourself. Have you ever heard the saying, "Put your own oxygen mask first"? This is a good reminder to stay in a calm state. If you are able to learn to remain calm when your child is distressed and show them the appropriate response, they'll learn to manage the issue. You could be an instrument of sound, but

should you become too stressed yourself it isn't helping them to get themselves. Be sure to pause before responding. Be honest and calm, let your child sort out his anger and direct him to what he must do. Be attentive and do not prolong the issue by engaging in a flurry of indulgence.

5. Be aware that triggers pass down over generations. It is possible to deactivate your buttons by understanding that this heightened sensitiveness you feel has been passed on to you by the generations and isn't as unique as you believed it to be. Most of the time, it was the hot button of your mother since it's her favourite and it goes on. Once you are free of your triggers, they'll be less of a problem for you, and as consequently and less of a concern to your kids. It will be easier for you all to understand the problem that is "sensitivity" for certain hot buttons in the proper perspective. Your entire family will be benefited.

Chapter 6: Taming Tantrums

Every parent has to fight struggles to control their toddlers' tantrums. It's an inevitable thing during the early years, and in particular between the ages of 1-4. Your child may be enjoying himself, and the next moment the child is screaming and yelling like a raging ball. He throws his body and screams as he lashes out as well as bites. The child doesn't realize that he has hurt other people and doesn't show the slightest amount of regret following the incident. The reason for this is because the display of temper is beyond his comprehension, and he is only acting out to express his anger or displeasure about something he wants in the present.

A. Understanding the Causes of Fits of Rage

There are a variety of reasons toddlers throw tantrums. In essence, it's the way he communicates with you, or others who are around him. He doesn't have a proficiency in the language therefore, your child relies on his body to ask for attention, satisfy his requirements, or to cope with the difficulties which come his way.

The most frequent causes of tantrums are:

* Hunger, fatigue, sickness, boredom, overstimulation, or physical discomfort

Each of these can trigger the child to throw a tantrum. The tantrum is the child's cry for help or a simple "enough". Because he doesn't know how to express his feelings the way he wants to, he reverts to what can be done: screaming, whining and lying on the ground with arms flailing, throwing objects and other irritating actions. There are instances when temper screaming fits result from physical issues that include chronic digestive issues and pain-inducing acid reflux. Therefore, keep an eye on it.

* Frustration

The child's anger is triggered by frustration which can lead to temper anger and tantrums. Children are naturally curious and like to explore or try to do whatever is observed by others. But, since he's in a state of weakness or uncoordinated and uncoordinated, it causes him to be frustrated. Since he's not able to keep his temper in check He gets angry, displays aggression, or engages in antisocial behavior.

* Search to be noticed

Young children want lots of attention and will do anything to the level of facing consequences, rather than being disregarded from their family members.

* You must be self-sufficient

As small as they may be toddlers can make parents uncomfortable by doing whatever they'd like to do. A tantrum is a method to assert their independence and gain control over their surroundings which can lead to conflict among them as well as their caregivers. After discovering there are limits and boundaries that they must adhere to, they will resort to throwing tantrums in protest.

* He isn't getting what he wants.

Children do not have a lot of control over their urges and wants; they are conditioned to believe that the adults around them to give whatever they desire.

This is why your child is having difficult time directing his anger when you do not fulfill his demands. He doesn't understand the reason you say "no" as well as "later." It is because he would like the item now and doesn't grasp the notion of delayed pleasure.

* Changes

Big or small changes and changes can upset toddlers. Anything that disrupts his planned schedule or routine can make him feel overwhelmed or emotional lost.

* Testing

The toddler age is when the child's understanding of the power that he is able to use over other people. He is constantly testing the boundaries and limits and experimenting with behaviors to help him achieve what he wants.

* Curiosity

He is trying to understand details about his surroundings, and is interested in the sounds and sights. Sometimes, because of the curiosity of his heart, he may do things that are not considered acceptable behaviour and could put his safety at risk.

Don't be shocked when your cat pulls his tail the cat, bangs on the table or uses crayons to draw across the room.

Additional important information about tantrums:

It's normal behavior for toddlers.

Beware of extreme tantrums that is violent, destructive that can occur up to 5-10 times per day, or lasts for more than 10 mins. It could indicate an issue with the underlying cause that requires help from a professional.

It is usually in children between the two and three years old.

It can be an indicator of an internal-focused disorders like anxiety or depression, which is typically easy to overlook in active toddlers.

* It could be a part of an outward-focused behaviour pattern, which causes the child to display an excessive amount of aggression, including destruction of objects or hurting others and himself. When this occurs, then he could be suffering from ADHD. (ADHD).

If you've figured out the different causes of tantrums, you can prepare in advance to prevent (or limit) the likelihood of it happening. One method to analyze the patterns of his temper tantrums is to write down a journal and record whenever it happens, the place it happens, the type of behavior he exhibits as well as the triggers and how it ends and much more.

The prevention of tantrums

There isn't a foolproof method to avoid tantrums, as they're out of the reach of toddlers. However, you can help encourage positive behavior by using the following methods:

* Prepare ahead. Before running your outdoor chores, be sure your child isn't fatigued and hungry. If you are planning to wait in line, make sure you bring your child's favourite snack and toys that will keep him busy. Knowing what is likely to be expected will prepare him to be successful.

* Be consistently. Establishing a routine for the day helps your child what you want from him. Following the schedule is

crucial, as are your child's bedtime and nap time. Set simple and appropriate boundaries.

Note his positive behaviour. Rewarding your child by hugging him or praising his behavior when he's doing well increases his self-esteem and is eager for this extra focus. The more positive feedback received for the desired behaviour, the more likely it is that he will repeat it.

* Let the child make his own decisions. Do not let him say "no." When you wish to help him develop confidence and control allow him to make his own choices in simple things like the kind of shoe he'd like to wear or the kind of fruit that he enjoys eating. Let him decide what that he would like to engage in and have him play with him frequently.

Beware of situations that could cause temper anger. Stay clear of places that could make him want to buy treats or toy if you're not planning to buy him one. If he's easily bored and wants to escape, steer him away from places that don't offer rapid service. Don't give the child toys that you think are complicated and complex with regard to age, or level of ability.

8 Tips to Deal with Your Toddler's tantrums in the public

Every parent has witnessed itwhen a child has an uncontrollable outburst in the public. What do you do in this situation?

Here are some strategies to control the screaming:

Strategies #1 - Be in peace and stay away from him.

If he does not physically threaten his safety or the safety of others or others, it is better to avoid him. Most toddlers will try crying and screaming to get parents to grant what they would like. It is crucial not to get angry.

Strategy #2 - The more loud you shout, the less you speak.

Maintain your calm and speak to your child with a calm, easy tone to calm your child. Try whispering softly to draw the attention of your child. This technique usually works because the child is trying to figure out what you're trying communicate, and he is forced to sit and able to listen.

Strategies #3. Don't be afraid to resist.

Accepting your toddler's demands and letting him get his own way is not a good option. It can cause the child to believe that acting out every time they want something is just a way to get something. Be firm and repeat the rules.

For example, you should not permit him to eat cookies prior to dinner. If he insists upon having one, and is throwing a fit then you can say "Cookies aren't allowed prior to dinner" over and over in a calm, neutral tone. As time passes when he stops whining, he will calm down and realize that you are in fact doing business.

Strategie #4 - Stay clear of the possibility of punishment in any way.

Be aware that the tantrum is just a symptom which will eventually be over. It is essential to be mindful and do not punish your child for throwing tantrums however annoying it may be. Your child is learning to manage and communicate. He is still unable to comprehend the reason he doesn't get all the things he desires. Beware of spanking, shouting and other punitive actions.

Strategie #5 - Empathize the child.

A small outburst could be an indicator that your child is experiencing that they are not acknowledged or heard. It is better to spot the issue early to prevent the situation from turning into an outburst that is full of anger. The best approach is to sympathize with his emotions, letting him feel that you are with him and wish you could allow or grant him the things he wants. Explain to him the reason you are unable to. It is possible to suggest another option.

Strategy #6: Take an air of freshness.

If your child is screaming for help Take him outside for some fresh air. A change in the environment can help calm a crying child.

Strategy #7: Have a fun game and make him laugh.

Engage your child with a simple game such as "I I" and "hide-and-seek," but make sure that your child is in eye-level, especially in an open space. For instance, you could hide and then disappear quickly between a clothing rack before reappearing with a gentle boo. If your child is happy and having fun, it helps keep the tantrums at bay.

Strategy #8 - Keep the person in close proximity without saying any word.

If no amount of reason or disinterest isn't enough to stop your child in his tears, the most effective solution is to just hug him. In this panic-inducing moment the child doesn't know or even see the person you are hugging. You must rely on the impact of your touch to calm the child and assist in restoring control. By picking up your child and holding him close and firmly will help him feel loved and respected. Sometimes, children need the security of a place where they can be able to calm their overwhelmed emotions.

Keeping Your Toddler Safe During Tantrum Display

If your child begins throwing, punching, or biting objects, or hitting, it is important to take the child away from the circumstances that cause the meltdown.

Choose your child with care and hold him tight to avoid injury, refrain from pulling or pulling. Choose a safe place for him to relax, allowing him to express his angry mood. The space he has is helpful in helping to manage his emotions, pulls him back together, and helps him regain control of himself.

Following the Tantrum

The child is the most at risk after a temper tantrum, therefore it is crucial to hug him to assure the child that he's loved, even if he has been behaviour. When he's calm, praise him for regaining control of his behavior by telling your child, "I like how you have calmed down." Do not give him the things he desires following the chaos. Be sure that he gets some rest and sleeps to heal from the dramatic incident.

When should you seek a doctor's Intervention

These tantrums are getting more frequently and intense, lasting longer than normal.

* The child starts to injure himself and others.

* The tantrums are often accompanied by feelings of fear, helplessness sadness, anger or extreme separation anxiety. sleeping problems, or a refusal to eat.

* The child fights often, doesn't agree, and can be very irritable.

Tantrums can cause an argument with your child.

You're beginning to be concerned about health issues that could cause the temper tantrums.

It is difficult dealing with the child's temper or calming your anger.

B. Don'ts and Don'ts If your children don't pay attention to what You're Doing

If your child is a confident, you will know. He has a more complicated personality, and is more likely to doubt your instructions or take your instruction. If you request for something, he will not listen. Then you repeat it but he continues to refuse to listen. It's a typical situation for parents of children who do not listen which is why parents are forced to have their children go to time-out or other discipline methods.

Did you know that human beings are wired in a way to be antagonistic? Everyone is influenced by a counter-will, which affects his reluctance when someone attempts to control or coerce him. This is an instinct that could be irritating at times for the parents. However, it helps keep children safe from people who have bad intentions.

The Reasons Kids Don't Listen

* Listening ability is a learned habit. If you don't train your child to pay attention to what's being spoken, he won't be able to listen. Training starts as early as the age of infancy, and you will teach your child that there is a "yes" or "no" of a variety of things.

• The kid is engaging in something things that interest him and is enjoying himself. If you insist that he perform a task while he's doing something he enjoys, he's likely to be ignoring you. If you speak without first gaining his attention, he'll not pay attention. Request him to stop whatever is going on and keep eye contact prior to you begin talking.

* What you would like him to do isn't pleasant or enjoyable for him, and the kid isn't interested in you. The pressure you place on your child to perform something that's not suitable for him, causes tensions and conflicts that cause him to avoid your presence.
* You are prone to giving long lectures , and then keep speaking and preaching. You don't take in what the person is trying to block or stop him from making suggestions or making comments.
* Avoid using words that your child doesn't like for example "Don't," "Can't," "No," "If," "Why," and "You." If you begin your remarks by using "You," it makes him feel snubbed, and you're making him feel like you are pointing fingers at him. The "If" phrases can put him in danger. When he is exposed to these words, he will turn off from what you're saying.
* You make a fuss. If you continue to repeat your instructions not only multiple times, but repeatedly your child may find you boring.

* You must not follow through with what you claim to do. You should be an example to your children. If your child sees that you are not paying attention when your spouse speaks to you, he's likely to be the same. Keep in mind that your child is constantly watching and mimicking your actions.

Another interesting reason why children aren't listening. Based on the study of 2013 by the American Academy of Pediatrics, children who are glued for an average of eight hours each all day in front television, computer, smartphone and other electronic devices reduce the vestibular sense as well as the proprioceptive signals that is essential for listening, sitting still and paying attention. These senses develop during playing outdoors or in outdoor activities. The most optimal time for the development of their senses to be rapid and efficient occurs before the age of six.

It is the one which connects all essential senses of the human body. It helps the child to know the position of his body in relation to his surroundings and comprehend the concept of balance. If it's not well developed, others senses are going to have a tough working at their maximum degree. This is the reason children tend to fidget or become aggressive, have more accidents, are easily overwhelmed, struggle with focus or listening or getting too close to others while engaging in conversations.

Here are a few activities that help to develop vestibular sense

Skating, swimming or jumping rope spinning, dancing around on a swing using a Merry-Go-Round or climbing trees, cartwheels, wheel-barrel walks or somersaults, turning upside down, bouncing backwards or with monkey bars.

Proprioception tells you where organs are situated without having to look at them. It is a sense that is connected to gravity perception which is the reason your child is able to put popcorn in his mouth, and not look away from the screen of the TV. Insufficient proprioception can cause a child to fall when climbing stairs , or slip out of the chair at mealtime or push too the limits when playing.

Here are some suggestions to aid in the development of proprioception:

Chewing, hugging or squeezing a stress ball and playing Tug-O-War using the stretch band, pulling or pushing a the wagon, raking leaves clearing snow and carrying buckets of sand or water, riding a trampoline and mixing Play Doh, building a fort by picking up and placing down large sticks, carrying boxes or lifting them.

It is essential to nurture the child's abilities by letting him engage in physical activities outside. At least three hours of exercise outdoors can be beneficial to their growth.

What should you do and what to avoid?

1. Don't think of discipline as a punishment. It is helpful to keep an open-minded attitude when disciplining your child and view the discipline as an effective way to build the morality of their character. It is essential to teach children self-control and control of their strong emotions. Take advantage of it as an

opportunity to get involved in his everyday activities.

In order to make your kids be attentive to your voice, make appeals to their "want-to" desires instead of insisting that he has to do it. It is better to allow him to choose his own options and help him become more cooperative instead of simply following your commands.

Make positive suggestions instead of negative instructions.

"Walk please" rather than "Don't take a run!"

"Kind hand Kindly, please," instead of "Stop hitting your brother!"

2. Discover open doors for applause. If you notice your child doing well or behaving properly, you should immediately applaud the effort. When he speaks to you about something pay attention to him. Be sure to show that you are in agreement with him when you feel it's appropriate, however, you should also be able to disagree when believe it's not safe to say so. When you are saying "no," it is crucial to state the reason for your disagreement.

3. Create boundaries. Limitations are essential to ensure that your child is safe or is acting appropriately. Once you've established the boundaries, you need in order to enforce them if they are breached. But, be careful not to impose punitive penalties that could compromise the physical and mental development.

Chapter 7: Techniques To Discipline Your Toddler

Like most parenting situations there isn't a universal way to discipline toddlers. The more tools for discipline that you can use, the more effective. Parents of toddlers may discover how much they depend on a single strategy the less effective this method is. Try these methods and pay on your child's reactions. Try to be as consistent as you can however, be flexible when your preferred method isn't effective anymore.

You can make use of the energy and passion your child is putting into a petty act and apply it to help others. For instance, if your child throws sand at a friend, you could remove your child from his sandbox, and provide the ball instead. So, your toddler continues to do something that he would like to perform (throwing) but you've transformed the negative into something positive.

Distraction

Redirection is similar to distraction,. However, instead of engaging in similar activities, select ones which aren't related to or contrary to the behaviour your child is showing. For instance, if your child is grabbing at an untidy strand of the living room rug , and you're worried that he'll break it, you could create the activity of painting with fingers within the chair. This provides your toddler with something enjoyable to do, and also gives you the opportunity to fix or take the rug off to be able to fix it later. This approach is ideal for actions that aren't necessarily inappropriate, but which others or you might find irritating. It's not the most effective option for serious behavior or repeated offenses that require more attention.

We are ignoring

The act of ignoring can be challenging to do However, it is extremely efficient. Sometimes, bringing attention to an undesirable behaviour can have the effect of aggravating the situation.

If, for instance, you're not usually swearing however, you happen to swear once and your child does it again and you don't let it go, just take it off your list. It's unlikely to repeat except if you create a major celebration of the incident.

If siblings are having a fight and no one gets injured, avoid getting involved so that they can improve their problem-solving abilities together.

It's also possible to end numerous temper tantrums when your child realizes that you're not able to give back the same violent reaction. Always ensure that she's secure and ignore the behavior that is causing the concern.

Natural Consequences

Some inconvenience as well as discomfort could be an instructive tool and isn't in any way abusive when you employ common sense. Allow your child to experience the consequences of his actions as often as you are able. Do not omit your child's every sorrow or attempt to make things simple. Be aware of these teaching moments. Most of the times, you will not even need to do anything for it to be effective. You can reinforce it by saying: "I asked you to take your toy several times, but you didn't do it and now it's in the hands of your grandmother until the it's time."

The Not-So-Natural Effects

It doesn't need to be naturally occurring to work, but you must be cautious. Check to see if your child is beginning to understand causes and effects independently at first. Some parents aren't a fan of this method since it can feel like punishment. It's more like receiving a speeding penalty. There's a standard that applies and if you do not follow it, you'll have to pay a penalty and might even lose the privilege to drive. It's not long for kids to grasp this. Be fair and consistent.

Make use of "If-Then" phrases. "If you steal your child's toys away from him, you'll be required to leave the area," or "If you continue to throw rocks at the window , then we're going to the inside."

Removing privileges or toys when it is motivating your child. "You can't play Dora today until you are dressed."

Time Out

Time out can work as a method for your child to take a break in the event of a temper screaming tantrum. It also helps him not be a nuisance or behave in the way you'd prefer. The objective is to assist him understand how to manage his own behavior . This approach can be very effective.

Use this method when your child displays outward anger or is not in control. Tell them, "I can't understand you when you're screaming," or "I understand your anger however, you must relax." After that, physically guide the child into a designated time-out area where he can return to you once he has regained control.

It is also possible to use short times of silence after you have given your child a warning for their behavior . Over time, he will realize that your rules are crucial and will make better decisions.

Tools for Toddler Discipline

The discipline of a toddler can be difficult however it is vital.

It is a challenging moment when trying to establish toddler discipline. Making sure that children know the difference between right and the wrong side at this young stage is challenging, yet crucial. Here are some resources to help you in this journey.

1. Guide little hands

Hands that are curious always look for things to touch Therefore, teach the little explorationist word associations to help him determine what he might handle. Consider using "yes touch" for things that are safe; "no touch" for objects not permitted and "soft touching" for animals and faces. To control the graber who is impulsive you can try to encourage "the one-touch touch." Other words (e.g. hot touch and Owie touch) will pop up when you explore all the possibilities of touching.

2. Little grabbers are to be respected.

Your child has an olive jar and you are imagining that it will soon be an unclean mess to tidy up. You rush to grab the jar out of her grasp in just a few seconds, and you've started an angry tantrum. You've gotten yourself out of a mess to tidy off the floor, but now you're faced with an emotional mess that you must care for.

There's a better approach. If your child is young look at her and distract her from something else she's interested in. If you have a more mature toddler inform her that you'll help her to open the jar so that she can take an olive and indicate where you would like her to place it. This is just an exercise in respect and politeness and respect, and an "adult-in charge" method. Children require adults to communicate and show the behavior that adults would expect.

3. Be a part of the world of your child

Children do things that are annoying in no way maliciously however, they do not consider themselves to be adults. You're likely to be miserable when you let every child-made mess make you feel. As you step into the kitchenarea, you notice your toddler at the sink spilling water all over the floor. It is possible to fall into the "poor me" mindset: "oh, no! Now I need to take care of the mess. Why is she doing this in my face?" Here's a healthier alternative. Instead of focusing on your own discomfort, take your child's perspective: "This is fun. Consider all the various activities you can perform with dishware and drinking water." Keep in mind that what she's doing is appropriate for her development. She's learning and exploring. Be aware that since two-year-olds can get so involved in their activities and are likely to be agitated when you attempt to get rid of her. If you put off an hour or so and she'll be off to do something else. And aside from that, water cleans easily; there's no problem. It won't happen again after she's reached the age of six. You'll see yourself smiling. Moving away from self and into your child's life saves mental stress. There's no need to tidy up the mess that has formed in your head, and also the water that has accumulated on the floor.

4. Divert and distract

Your 1-year-old is stumbling towards the lamp's cord. Instead of grabbing him and risking a tantrum Begin by grabbing his attention by using his name or other word you've learned can make him stop in his tracks for long enough to keep him from. After that, you can quickly redirect him to a safer option. For instance in the past, when Lauren was younger when she'd get into trouble, we'd shout "Lauren!" Hearing her name caught her off guard and caused her to temporarily forget what she was trying to accomplish. When we caught the attention of Lauren, we'd swiftly divert her attention prior to her putting an enormous amount of energy in her original plan.

5. Provide redirectors

A baby's brain is brimming with thousands of word connections. One of the patterns of association we observed in Matthew's development diary was that whenever I'd say "go" to the 16-month old Matthew he would grab his babysling and rush towards the front door. If we observed Matthew heading for a major mischief, we would say "go." That signal could be enough to prompt his body and mind to alter direction. We kept an alphabet of cues to use to serve as "redirectors" ("ball," "cat," "go," and like that).

6. Limits Set

A lot of your discipline is contingent on your ability to establish boundaries. Humans need boundaries and the more young the child, the clearer will be the boundaries. The boundaries provide protection for the child whose curious nature allows him to explore, however his lack of experience could make him wander off. Think about the famous test: Once the schoolyard fence was taken down in the middle of the day, the kids were free to roam throughout the property were confined to the middle of the yard, hesitant to venture into the previously fenced-in spaces. The boundaries do not restrict children, but instead protect the curious child and the surrounding area, allowing the child to be more productive within the confines of those boundaries. For instance, your child does not want to hold your hand when you cross the parking lot or street. It is a strict rule to ensure that the street or parking lot crossings are only permitted with hands held. There's no alternative. We worked tirelessly to find the ideal balance between freedom and restrictions on our young children. It wasn't easy. We wanted them to gain knowledge about the world around them and about themselves however, not at the cost of hurting others or themselves. They were awed by rules and knew how to use them. When a rule had to be followed, they would frequently read the rule out loud for us to listen and then see whether it was still in effect.

Limit-setting is a great lesson in life The world is filled with yeses and no. You determine what behaviors you are not willing to tolerate and stick to your limits. It will differ for every family and level of growth. Limits can bring a whole new level of stress that every child has to be confronted with on the family front before being confronted by it beyond the door. You decide that you do not want your child to waste time and so you put the lid on the trash bin closed. The doors to the pantry locked since you don't want shelves to be emptied in a hurry. Make him stop pulling on the dog's fur and instruct the dog to pat it gently. Sharp knives and scissors are not allowed. They are taught to stay out of reach and you are able to "distract and replace" in the event of an emergency. Setting limits can benefit the whole family. The child must learn how to live with all the family members and parents must be open about their limits. One mother said, "I know her limits--and mine too."

Many parents don't limit their children's abilities because they don't want to be able to watch their child unhappy. A healthy dose of anger can let a baby experience just the right amount resistance that keeps him striving to his maximum potential. No frustration, no growth. No life, no frustration. You must model the proper way to deal with the frustration. Adults also have their limits. If you're able to handle your limits then you'll know how to set boundaries for your child.

Toddlers are looking for an adult to set boundaries for them. Without limits, the world becomes too frightening for their children. They instinctively know that they require the safety that limits provide. When they push the limits, they're asking you to demonstrate the trustworthiness of you and what your limits are.

7. Take the initiative

As each of our children entered the toddlerhood stage and we began to think about our authority roles. We wanted to be clearly in charge of our children to ensure that they felt secure and safe with someone who was there to protect them from all the risks of the world, as well as the ability to reach out for assistance. We didn't want to make them as puppets in order we could feel strong. Contrary to the belief of certain theorists, our family were not convinced that our toddlers were trying to be in control of us. They were the ones who desired to master. We assisted them by two methods. One, we let them know through our voice and the way we behave as mature adult. Second, by providing them with as a secure and safe home base that they are able to leave and return to feel safe and secure. By doing this we could assist them to create their own internal controls.

8. Create the structure

If your child is the age of one and reaches one year old, a new name is added to the parenting job description: the architect of your child's world. When you take on this role, you guide your child's attention towards enjoyable learning experiences and away from danger. You establish structure, which doesn't mean that you are rigid or controlling. What we refer to by "structure" is creating the conditions for positive behavior. Structure guards and redirects. The child is free to be a kid and give them the chance to grow and become mature. A structured environment is a good one for children. Through a bit of planning you eliminate the majority of "no's" in order to create you have a general "yes" atmosphere prevails.

The structure of the environment is altered as the child grows. Through all stages of development, changing the environment of your child is among your most effective ways to discipline your child. As your child reaches the grasping stage and you're careful to place your coffee cup away from the reach of your child. If your toddler is able to access the bathroom, you begin locking the lid or shutting the door of the bathroom. The child who is unable to go to bed at night enjoys the time to relax before bed. The nine-year-old who struggles to complete her work gets a quiet comfortable and inviting place to work from and also has the strictest restrictions on TV at school. The structure sets the stage for positive behaviors to prevail over unwanted ones.

Chapter 8: Toddlers and Siblings

How do you deal with Your Toddler as well as Your New Baby

If we have a child, we've got all the time in the world to push to know their needs, recognize their desires and meet their requirements and witness them grow with each new stage of their growth is exciting and new especially when they're the grandchild with the most They get plenty of adult time and spotlight. When you have a second child you will notice a lot of adjustments to your routine and your family. It may be overwhelming at first. Once you know the emotions your toddler might experience and, as a result the changes to your parenting. Once you've gotten this down, you'll feel more at ease handling the two children in your family.

First-borns naturally draw a lot of attention.

With all the attention and focus we often jump when the baby starts crying. We respond immediately to their needs make sure they are clean and tidy, show the new skills to do in a proper manner and then encourage a similar from them. Many toddlers are first born and prefer tidy hands, all things placed in the right spot and needs addressed immediately and the skills that mom and pop have exactly as the routine that is followed in accordance with the guidelines! (when they require the routine).

The second baby is likely to become more flexible

We then have a second child and things change, and then we don't have the energy, time, or motivation to make everything be perfect and certainly doesn't mean we want to get it done in a hurry! As moms, we're having to take care of and managing two kids now and something needs to be given.

It is important to prioritize and then naturally become more flexible, and learn what we need to do when we have the time. In the process of prioritizing, we are prone to take care of the loudest first. As a result, the child with the next is likely to discover that how flexible they are. They've have to wait for a meal and hear the voice of mommy and be assured that mom is likely to show up at some point, much like twins who quickly learn that mom will soon be here.

As a parent of a toddler as well as an infant, the child is often pushed around and wants to go ways to rest in different locations because the toddler has developed an activity routine and routine. Mom wants her toddler to have their routines and routines and in order to establish a sense of living a normal life with the addition of a baby has arrived. It can help promote a flexible sleep pattern for the newborn baby, and many moms have reported that their second child is more flexible. the reason why the second child has more flexibility is because mom was much more flexible, and also less stressed about everything. Then the baby responds in a similar way.

It's a good idea to recall that your toddler has been through several years of strict rules that everything was done the way they've asked for it, and rules are followed and a lot of focus. As the baby has arrived Mom might have loosened the rules and become more flexible as there's a lot more to be able to however, your toddler wants all things to be identical.

They aren't aware or comprehend that the rules might be changing because you're more busy and believe that your needs must be immediate responses like they did prior to. This is the reason why toddlers have difficulty adapting into the brand new infant and require more attention.

Follow the routine of the toddler.

It is crucial to take care of your toddler's routines and follow them for eating , sleeping, and playing at the same time. Your toddler needs to be to be met in the fullest extent due to the arrival of a new baby. But, the newborn will become more flexible with regards to routine and in nature, toddlers at this age will be able to set time for eating, sleeping, and playing. As a result the child will have different awake and sleep times that aren't fixed to a clock. Thus, you'll be able to avoid trouble by making sure the toddler's routine is adhered to at first.

In particular, during the bustling late afternoon "arsenic time," the new baby will need regular feedings and shorter hours of sleep . It could also be a part of the toddler's preparation for bedtime routine. When the toddler is bed, allow the child an opportunity to unwind with a relaxing meal prior to going to sleep.

It's acceptable to encourage toddlers to cooperate and patience in this stage. Moms are more comfortable when they recognize that the toddler phase is concerned with "me," Therefore, the toddler is able to think on the concept of "what's going on for me?" Let's say we make all requests addressed to the toddler end with a reward (of time or an outing or an activity that they enjoy). In this scenario we're more likely to see co-operation because as the child gets older. Positive encouragement will keep them engaged.

Learning to measure and playing with others

Even if the toddler seems to be a fan of the toddler, they'll likely love them! As parents we'd like to show how to interact with the baby, how to kiss them, washing their hands, gentle play and when to go into the nursery and look towards their faces (poke at them).

Your toddler isn't aware of what they are doing or how to behave and may feel off-putting if any contact with your baby is resisted or looked on. Keep in mind that your toddler has an extremely limited concentration span, so provide some cuddles and time with the baby and then after a few minutes, they'll move on to something other. Make sure you read when you're on the couch feeding your baby, and make sure you spending time with your toddler as soon as your child has some playing on the floor or is back in the bed.

How can you influence the sibling rivalry in Toddlers

Sibling rivalry can be a normal, natural circumstance because every child wants to have the father and mother by himself. If parents are planning to be a judge and intervene. However, the arguments are only a matter of time and make the children get more angry.

Your children will be able to win their fights and discover how to win, negotiate and respect their strengths, and each child will play the useless, misunderstood wimp and, as a result the mean, savage bully. The less parents intervene, the less children hurt one another and, consequently, the less likely they are to be enslaved to the roles that is "bully" as well as "wimp."

Sibling battles are a great way to prepare for the world of work. If you let your children know that you trust them to develop their own relationships, the best result will be a caring loved and treasured one. Your children will also gain confidence as well as self-esteem.

While you're away from your children's interactions does not mean that you avoid their emotions. As parents, they have the responsibility to help their children express and comprehend their feelings.

You do not want them be a victim of being a victim of "bad" emotions.

Keep in mind that children are allies within every family. Moms need to be firmly on one side and that is, the children should be are on the other side.

Help him learn to share and Aid Siblings

Birth of a second baby can be a massive transition for your child however it can be difficult to be aware of this, especially when we're the ones up all the night. When we're in those situations (if we're not exhausted to think about it) It is usually beneficial to imagine OUR lives and relationships becoming abruptly and drastically altered.

So here are some helpful tips to help your toddler adapt to and befriend their new baby sibling:

BEFORE YOU BABY IS BORN:

1. Engage in bonding with you"and your 'listening belly' Even as you'll begin to form bonds with your child even before they are born and your toddler can be aware that the soon-to-be-born sibling will

already hear them in your stomach. This can be a wonderful way to have interactions when you're talking, reading or noting music while playing with your child, for example, "your sister and that you are about to finish reading this book and you'll be able to hear it through my belly when you start the book, we'll be ready to show you pictures as well" or "I am wondering if you would like that song as well - your brother chose this song to let us all listen to."

After the birth of your baby:

Make sure you are prepared for baby gifts The majority of people are very generous when they have a baby. However, toddlers are often neglected. Put the baby's toys away and let them open after hours or stock a few boxes of gift wrappers that you're happy to take to your child if they seem to be struggling with this.

Encourage your toddler to help in other ways: this doesn't mean giving a bath or placing the baby down (although it can be tempting on certain days) However, your child can be asked to assist by other means, for example, "which does one think is a better outfit for your little sister today? This or the other? Thanks for helping".

If you have a useful toddler reception is definitely able to help you avoid using nappies, wipes, or wipes. Or helping you rub your baby's hands together.

Controlling feeding time As you're aware infants, who are born, require long to eat during from the beginning days to weeks. frequently, mothers find it to be a challenge to communicate with their children while still being able to feed their children at the same time.

It is a good idea to make an assortment of "special feeding activities' that can only be made during the feeding time. The box will contain several new puzzles, toys, or even books. It's all focused on creating an positive relationship with the infant in the brain of your toddler. If your toddler is fond of books eating time is an ideal time to have your child snuggled up to your arms while your baby feeds the other and reading a book.

Know the motivations that drive your toddler's behavior Certain toddlers are eager to express their feelings through the form of words while others communicate their feelings through their behavior. It can be a stressful period for your child and although they do have their limits however, they need your attention.

Enjoy this stage as it is: Finally Enjoy this life stage there will be days where it appears as a significant achievement that you've made it however, I'm convinced that nobody ever is laying on their deathbed wish they had more rest, instead, it's more likely that people look back at these years and wish they had loved them.

Chapter 9: Children's Discipline Tips for Parenting'

A firm stand is not a bad aspect for parents to master. Children need discipline. They learn what constitutes acceptable behavior and what's not. In some cases training is essential to helping children achieve outcomes. Make it short, concise and pay attention to the child's opinions. It's not about grabbing the child or demeaning them. It's about leading the group to teach them appropriate behavior in a legal manner, shrewd and secure way. In the case of such a high amount of guardians, there is a fear of squeezing a child's soul or overwhelming them with the excessive amount of cutoff points, have them sit backwards in an arrangement in the order train only to be viewed by inconsiderate, reckless and rude children for a long period of time.

Children do not only require boundaries; they require them. It helps them feel safe and even loved. They're still not able to figure out how to manage their desires and desires yet, and they look to you, as a parent, as a model for showing the behavior that is acceptable, and what's not. Order is more than just an device to create respectful children It's a tool for make balanced and truly healthy children.

The right kind of schedule could be among the toughest tasks a parent has to accomplish. Every child is unique and while breaks can work well for one child, a different one might require a gentle tapping of the back to indicate what's in your account. In order to help you get the most probable arrangement for the issues that arise at home, adhere to these important tips from the master of youngster development T. Berry Brazelton, M.D.

Take note of a child's stage of Development.

Knowing why your kid is always playing in the sand, even though you've told them repeatedly could allow you to more likely plan your displeasures and discover the cause of whether your kid isactually not obeying, or simply looking into their lives in a healthy and normal manner.

Adjust the discipline to the Child's Stage of Development.

Babysitters are usually without much enjoyment, while older children might require breaks or other forms of discipline to force them to stop what they're working on. Find out the best approach for each stage of development of a child for more effective outcomes.

Choose a discipline that is appropriate for the child.

All you had be able to do is shake your head her to express your displeasure then she started crying without control and then stop her actions. But not with my child. He often insists that his behavior isn't acceptable to you, therefore you need to enforce a stricter method of instruction to teach the off-base. Don't use the same method of controlling for every child. Chances are that it will be effective for a small portion of children and not the rest.

Do your best to be a role model.
If your child notices that you are irritable whenever you don't follow your particular way, consider how they'll react. Teach your kids how to manage discontent and disappointment. Be an effective role model.
Always show children love and tenderness. The moment when discipline is over. Whatever the situation, whether it's at

home by themselves or tapping their hands to your child, always embrace them and reinforce the fact that you cherish them, even the fact that they are resistant. It's reassuring to know that you're the most important person in the eyes of your parents regardless of how you mess up.

There are a few significant consequences to inflexible physical discipline (forceful behavior, fear and minor) Some guardians have realized that taking an energizing and steady stance (in the most delicate and loving manner) will often result in better results than talking breaking, over-clarifying or breaks would. What's more how do you know that you've proved to be overly demanding and intolerant? Be aware of these indicators:

A child who's tranquil and peaceful because they're reluctant to commit an mistake.

A child who is too sensitive to even the smallest amount of analysis.

A pitiful tyke.

A child that exhibits symptoms of pressure that ranges from moderate to extreme.

A child who is experiencing relapses in his conduct (potty making and freedom, resting in a problematic way etc.).

If you spot any of these indicators you might have the perfect time to loosen up and review the most effective method of training and correct your child's poor behavior.

Parents of Toddlers

If you're the parent of a baby you are aware of how draining life can be when you live on an everyday basis. Your baby could be as cute as a bug at one point and then rapidly transform into a beautiful terror just a few minutes later. There are some basic parenting techniques that you can employ to assist in making your life gradually more sensible for toddlers and young children.

It is vital to understand how to raise your children with respect and to ensure that both you and your kids will be happier and productive. Instead of getting overwhelmed by the responsibilities and challenges that keep popping up, parents must realize the concept that "picking your parenting battles with grace" is an excellent general advice. Simply focus on your needs and demands and work out ways to take advantage of this amazing time spent with your kids.

Making preparations

When you realize that you must watch out for your child (or the puppy could end with a shaded coat as a result of the new application of an permanent marker) it is likely to be difficult to complete your task, such as keeping the house under order, making healthy meals and the sky's the limit. To ensure that the rest of your home running smoothly it is crucial to prepare your meals.

One method to ensure you have good dinners and snacks ready in a short amount in time would be to chop into pieces your items from the soil after returning to your home after a trip to the market. In addition, by creating an entire meal that is twofold and putting one-third of the meal into the cooler to be used later for to use, without worrying about having to set it up again.

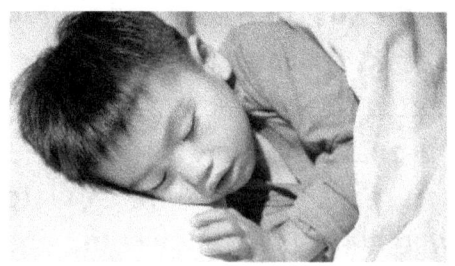

When you vacuum, do your clothes and other household chores as your child goes to bed to sleep every day, the home is also kept in good order. If you work from home then this is the perfect opportunity to get familiar with the phone calls that require an unflappable family unit to make the task.

Control

Sometimes the most difficult thing about being a parent is the constant requirement of an instruction. This is the time that your precious child discovers how to feel confident out without warning, and pushes any limits using the feared words, "No!" Your toddler must be delicate but solid, so that he is aware exactly where the breaking points are, and there are outcomes every time you cross the limit. If you are dependable Your child will soon realize that there are opportunities within the limits, and will gradually cease pushing against them frequently as possible.

In the end, as toddlers can in general be debilitating It is essential to make an investment when the situation becomes difficult. It's okay to let your child screaming in a room and let yourself relax and regroup prior to returning to apply discipline.

Help your toddlers develop self-reliance regardless of how much could be anticipated. You'll get some time off and your child will enjoy being able to exercise additional independence.

Tips for Parenting the Toddler

Toddlers can be a challenge but could also be a amount of fun when you are aware of what they are thinking. Finding the most effective devices and systems to aid to get through the toddler years is all you need to enjoy this short time. Be aware that a and later they'll go on to the next stage, with a variety of challenges for you.

There are numerous parenting advice to teach your child. The list is never ending. However there are a few of basic rules that could be very useful.

Five of my best ways to teach your toddler the right way to be. With these standards teaching your child will be much more simple.

Make sure your child gets enough time to rest. We are far better when we've been able to sleep. Take note of the way you feel when you're exhausted. It's hard to concentrate You think you're a mess and try as best you can but in some instances, you're not able to function properly.

Toddlers adapt so regularly. They'll appreciate it more and have more fun when they get enough time off.

Be sure to get enough sleep. This is a self-explanatory. It is possible to reconsider your family's sleeping habits and the schedules that go along to that may take a few minutes to convince it to be healthy. However, the benefits are going to be worth it, despite all the hassle. The way you and your child believe in your beliefs will influence your beliefs and thoughts and, ultimately, what you do to your child.

Have realistic expectations for yourself and your child. This means they are aware of the development capabilities of your child. Sometimes we may expect much from them, but they're not fully prepared for it. Sometimes, we have unrealistic expectations of our parents too. Be cautious of yourself and keep in mind that the role of a parent is one of studying experience too. It is a job that you'll learn for an amazing amount of time.

Make sure you take care of yourself as a person not only as an adult. It's not difficult to get involved in simply becoming a parent. Some parents discover that, in a flash the toddler becomes the center of all they do. Keep in mind that you are a person as a whole. If you take your own care and taking in your child's development regularly, you'll feel refreshed. They'll be more valuable to you. It's similar to having a break away from your work. If you return to your activity, you feel more energized invigorated, excited and enjoy the experience more. It is crucial to model self-respect to your child. It also reflects self-esteem. If you don't value yourself, you shouldn't imagine that someone else would. Set an excellent example to your child and guide them to grow into confident, self-respecting adults.

Make sure you are a united front with your partner. If you support one another , it shows your child they aren't able to play off each other and undermine each of you states. If you do not agree with each other at the time, encourage one another and discuss it later. The toddlers are smart and learn to manipulate in every aspect immediately. Remember that they see you as above everything else and can figure out how to manipulate your catch to gain the things they want.

These are the parenting pattern strategies to teach your child. If you implement different methods to teach your child how to develop these skills techniques, they will surely to succeed because the nuts and bolts have been put in place.

Sleep Training Tips - Cheeky Chops

Before electricity, people's schedules could rise and set with the sun's light source and it was compatible with the natural rhythm of our clocks - at the time, many people slept the amount of sleep they needed. In our fast-paced life, our ability to maintain a sufficient amount of sleep isn't a thing of the past. Ask you where your rest on your list of priorities is?

This is a common occurrence for infants and kids because of the huge amount of classes and activities to be interested in, a lot of children, toddlers , and even Mum's are overwhelmed. Some of these classes clash with the tyke's innate plunge into sharpness, which means that normal nap times become more difficult to schedule. The need for sleep is greater in the the beginning stages than in any other age groups and the absence of restful sleep for children and infants is a threat in the development of emotional and physical well-being It shouldn't be viewed as a negative thing.

The most crucial test for parents is how to ensure a good night's sleeping for their children, If propensities are being infused into their children with the potential to influence changes in the child's behavior can seem overwhelming in the vast number of school of thought. Combine this with your own difficulty sleeping and the concept becomes overwhelming.

It is crucial to decide what is the best for your household and consider as a healthy sleeping routine to include and what you are comfortable with and don't like. Don't be compelled to change things from outside sources. Make the right choice with your family.

It's possible to change your mind with appropriate information and guidance - however, don't be expecting spectacular results in a short time - just be realistic. If your child is today have affiliations or multiple issues the process of preparing for sleep is a process of learning and is carried out in stages to allow the process to flow smoothly for all. It is a process that requires effort, imagination and most importantly, perseverance. Imagine trying to find a way to play a game that constantly changed the rules You'd never know the way to play the diversion Isn't it? Here's a summary of questions and suggestions to be aware of before making modifications to your household's sleeping habits.

Do you have a daily by calendar for your day? Children thrive with consistency. If you didn't know when that it would happen or when you'd next take a nap or eat - what would you feel?

What can you do to make your infant or tyke sleep? If your child wears braces (shaking the Mum or Dad's bosom, chest, and so on) while your child is asleep it is possible that they may experience short moments of illumination and will require similar conditions to go back to sleep. This result without sleep for everyone in any gathering that is. What would you think of yourself when you lay in your bed, comfortable and relaxed with your pillow and duvet and woke up in the front yard?

What is the best place for your infant to sleep? Find a spot in which your child can rest in a comfortable and secure lodging it is where they will spend the majority of things in mind and get all night to sleep. You should feel completely relaxed if your place of sleeping has changed. Vehicle - the lounge chair, the carriage, Sling?

What time will your kid get ready to go to sleep? Not getting your child's usual break is crucial in situations where you require a quick change. A tired child is often unbalanced and can be a challenge to resolve. Are you feeling sluggish at the end of your meal and then feel like you've got another wind later in the evening?

Does your kid snooze regularly? Take whatever steps necessary to even think about the importance of sleep during the day. If your child is continuously not getting enough rest, at this time their ability to adapt to their environment decreases, and then they are forced to are in a state of emergency. How do you adjust when you're exhausted after the hectic day and prepping dinner and the phone is ringing and the TV on, making plans for the next day and trying to keep an eye on the children? I'm sure that you are craving shoutingjust as a toddler.

Making adjustments to your child's or toddler's sleep routine should only be considered only when there are no other significant modifications are happening in order that you think and demonstrate your devotion. It's not logical for your baby or toddler to keep changing methods or strategies and this could cause confusion.

What is the best time to Transfer Toddlers to a Bed?

The bed was the initial space where one can sleep. The foundation at first was nothing more than open space in the earth. The most common type of bed for infants was supported. They were tiny and ideal for the newborn baby. Beds for children have a long story. They were probably one of the most essential household things brought in to a house as the reports on children were on the way.

In the 1800s, as homes grew, the bassinet was brought to be in order to provide the needs of growing children. They were typically custom made and then lowered from toddler to kid. Children's beds were also handed down to more current kids as most likely they were made using the solid wood from the region.

When is the right moment to remove your child from the den or support?

If you notice that your child is growing beyond its bed, it is time to shift the child to a larger bed. Many children prefer to sleep in large beds fast instead of sleeping in the bed's mattress. A bed is designed for babies and young children. There isn't a set rule to determine the best time to get the child from their home and into a home.

In general, the it is difficult to provide enough support for a baby in its third month. In order to help your baby sleep more peacefully it is possible to transfer your infant into an accommodation immediately. If your child is over the support level, now is a great time to shift the child who is in the issue to the bed.

As babies grow, they final stages, they begin to move around; when your baby is in the bassinet, it could cause danger to the tyke. Because little children don't understand the effects of gravity they aren't able to protect themselves from falling when the bassinet tilts.

Make sure you don't place any pads of toys that are stuffed into the bed with your child because they could pose a risk of a sudden newborn child developing disorder SIDS. If you place toys and pillows in the bed with a small child, they could be covered to the point of death. It is important to be careful when choosing the best infant bed so that you don't risk your infant while trying to make the right decision.

You could make the transition from a bed support to a bedroom more smoothly for your baby by making it for them to enjoy the distinct bed. It is possible to do this by allowing your child to have fun during the day as they look at you from the comfort of their home.

If you're looking for amazing ideas for blessings then you might want to think about one of the numerous baby blessing containers. You can find them online. You can choose and choose the type of endowments that you will need to include in the blessing bins you buy for your baby. You can pick a custom infant blessing bushel now. No matter if you're choosing a crate of blessings for an infant girl or a child infant You are certain to delight mommy of the baby with appropriate gifts for the baby in need!

Chapter 10: Physical and Mental Development

Physical Development
Bodily development is an essential area of development for children that is a part of kids' physical development and their increasing ability to control the muscles of their bodies. The physical development of children is based on a predetermined pattern however every child is growing according to their own cost. Active play is a great way for children to develop their motor skills. Baby care packages can aid the development of children's bodies by providing the best environment, safe environments, and ample time to play and explore.

Helping both Large Motor And Small Motor Development in Children's Care

The child care facilities are a important in helping children develop their motor skills. "Motor competences" is a vast class that encompasses a vast array of capabilities that range from sitting to running, climbing mountains, and from picking the right gadgets to writing using a pencil or pencil. Motor abilities generally fall into two types one of which is a large motor and a smaller. Baby care providers can help youngsters to develop every kind of motor skill.

Large Motor Skills

Large motor capabilities develop in a surprising manner in the first years of youth. The big motor abilities trigger the development of bigger muscle movements which are able to be utilized to jogging, jumping and throwing. As infants crawling, lifting the head and rolling or sitting down are all examples of improvement in gross motor. When children are 3 to five years old, examples of gross motor development include being able to running, hopping, and standing using one's feet, kick and throw the ball, climbto the top of the stairs or a playground -- and even trip on a tricycle.

Small Motor Skills

Small motor abilities require to the development of smaller muscles, mainly in the hands and fingers. The development of small motor abilities also involves hand-eye coordination. Small motor skills are accountable for preserving, greedy, and manipulating small objects. For example, small motor skills are needed to grasp an object like a crayon, hold it in a crayon, and then move it around the floor. Small motor abilities are crucial for threading beads and cutting them with scissors, or tie shoelaces. Before young children grasp these tasks they need to develop the strength of their fingers and hands and control through games.

Learning to Coordinate Large And Small Motor Skills

Although the larger muscles tend to expand before smaller muscle tissues, exceptional motor abilities require children to combine their huge motor skills with their smaller motor capabilities. The challenge of climbing up playground equipment requires them to use the huge muscles of their legs and arms to propel them upwards and forward. In the same time youngsters should utilize superior motor skills to coordinate hand and eye movements and also to alter how they grip the. Mountaineering kids need to coordinate the movement of various muscle groups in order to ensure the stability of their bodies.

Play Activities To Help Encourage Motor Development in Child Care

Play is crucial in the development of children's functional and satisfactory motor skills. Through play, children develop and master the control and coordination of huge body movements, and even small movements of arms and hands. Children's care providers can help children's motor development by planning play games that provide kids every day opportunities of moving their bodies.

Activities To Help Gross Motor Development

Gross motor skills include management of the legs, fingers and head as well as the trunk. Care providers for toddlers can assist kids develop their gross motor skills through the development of opportunities for their children.

run

bounce

hop

Throw and catch

to climb up, down, through, and over things

Tricycles that pedal or other trip-on toys

Push and pull

Fill and dump

The most unique sports that help gross motor development include running at high speeds as well as jumping rope, betting hopscotch, tossing and taking balls of all sizes, throwing bean bags, climbing in numerous unique rules, pedaling toy cars such as pulling carts or toys that push strollers, toy strollers or Brooms, filling and emptying buckets as well as various packing containers. Be aware that gross motor development takes place inside as well as outdoors. The crawling tunnel ride-on vehicle or pull toy may assist children to exercise huge movements of their legs and arms.

Activities To Help Fine Motor Development

The most effective motor abilities are based on the controlled manipulation of tiny muscles inside fingers, toes and arms and feet. The control of the muscles that allow the lips and tongue to speak or sing is also a great motor capability. Child care providers can design activities that help children build superior motor skills. Try some of the following activities that help with finger and hand coordination:

Play dough or clay using tools made of plastic, such as cutters for cookies or scissors to create various shapes

blocks of various sizes that you can stack and arrange

beads such as macaroni, rigatoni wheel-formed cereals to string onto shoelaces or yarn

puzzles that come with different length handles or knobs

Paints, scissors, brushes crayons, markers and massive chalk are all safe for infants.

Sharing your analysis is also the perfect opportunity to stimulate the development of motor skills. Engage children to demonstrate their ebook pages. Keep in mind that books with boards are ideal for children who are very young as the pages are stronger and easier to manage. Gross and excellent motor skills are essential tools that children use in the lecture hall as well as at home in the playground. Play is among the best ways to improve motor skills. If you give your kids enough chances to have fun with a range of thrilling substances, younger youngsters will discover a myriad of innovative and exciting strategies.

What can child care providers Expect from the physical development of toddlers

Baby care providers have a crucial role in promoting the physical development. The growth of children's bodies accelerate their growth during the period between twelve and thirty-six months. As they grow, babies go from studying to walk, to the point where they can run, climb, and soar with confidence. Children explore their environment by being able to touch, manage and taste the entire environment surrounding them. They develop from the simplest motor skills to the ability to flip pages in a book and draw using a pencil. They start to learn about bladder control and could be able to utilize the toilet. As the muscle tissues of their tongues and mouths grow, they become better in presenting phrases and use of language to communicate. When you are a child care provider you have a vital role in helping the development of children's physical abilities. The following list of lists outlines some typical motor and physical abilities that toddlers typically examine for a specific time. This list is only an idea of guiding principles. Each child is a woman or a man and is able to develop in accordance with her needs.

Between 12-18 months, the majority of toddlers

They weigh between 17 and 30 kilograms and stand between 27-35 inches tall.

I am able to be on my own, lie in a recliner and "cruise" or even as a shield directly from furniture

Begin walking and gradually more confident walkers thanks to years of experience

Are able to gesture or point at objects to suggest they're looking for?

Want to pull and push things, including strollers and carts, plush toys and even furniture

Enjoy filling and emptying containers for packing

Hats can be removed as well as socks and mittens.

It is possible to flip pages of the book's robust board

could begin to stack two blocks

Experiment with poking, twisting, and squeezing objects

could also be interested in flushing toilets, and last doorways

enjoy carrying small things while walking, often with one on each hand.

begin to keep the crayon and scribble, but struggle to control the scrawling

Let them wave goodbye and then clap their hands

You can choose smaller bite-sized snacks and take them to eat

Enjoy protecting the spoon when eating but could also experience difficulty getting it into the mouths of their guests.

Balls can be rolled to an adult if requested by

Mental Development

The development of mental abilities is an essential element of development, taking into account the various mental abilities. It begins right at the beginning as the child grows, his mental reactions also alter. These reactions are easy at first, but in the right direction, they create complex mental processes. Intellectual development encompasses such skills like observing, attending recalling, observing asking questions, solving problems and growing in intelligence, in addition to language. These abilities develop and get older and decrease as we older age. The value of alternates varies depending on age and the type of review. In spite of a certain pattern of intellectual development, every character is able to grow and develop in a specific way. The different intellectual skills or sports mentioned above are interconnected and are able to grow together. They're interconnected and can no ever increase by themselves. Apart from this, interdependence is a different characteristic of improvement in mental health is its consistency. Intellectual development is a different term to broaden the horizon of highbrow of the child. In the beginning the field is a large, "booming, humming confusion" for the child. Gradually, information is absorbed and comprehended, differences are discovered and evaluations and knowledge are organized to make new family members. This is possible through strategies of differentiation, as well as corporate or integration. The factors that influence intellectual development include the process of maturation, learning and education. The kind of nervous human brain that the infant acquires is a major aspect. It allows him to coordinate multiple sports and actions. It manages the activities of all the organs. The mind, which is an essential component of the apprehensive system is a bigger role in the mental development of a person than any other component. It assists to perceive the surrounding world, and the notion is the concept of mind - all thought and recognition.

The stages of mental development:

From the time of birth until three years old:

The baby has all the sensory devices that could be necessary for mental entertainment. At 3 years old He demonstrates the capacity to fulfill his desires in a selective manner. This is where his mental development begins. This is evident from various kinds of behavior. He is either secure or attempts to appear relax

Approval from his mother , father, and other family members for subjects he is attracted to or enjoys. A child's curiosity is an additional characteristic of the development of his mind at this stage. The child is curious about the world around him, as well as humans. Another proof is the kid's capacity to consider. He is a victim of illusion and is the personification of the technology around him. He is able to discern between himself and other people and has a tendency to be optimistic.

From Three to Six Years:

The first year of a child's life is marked by the ability to use the use of symbols and words. He is exposed to many perceptual and sensory experiences. these experiences contribute to the development of his brain.

Later Childhood:

This time is marked by the power to develop a clear and accurate idea. A clear and precise faith, comes the technique of conceptualization. Also, mental improvement can be seen by his growing interest. He is beginning to be respectful of the people around him. He starts to imitate the manners and behaviors of those they admire.

The many aspects of Mental Development:
Sensation and Perception:

Concept and sensation are the basis of intellectual growth. The sense is the first step towards understanding, but it takes the shape of information best when it is addressed and connected to it. In different words, feelings are made objectified, and they become significant. These sensations that are objectified are referred to as perceptions. In the beginning the environment of the child is an undifferentiated, indistinct mass due to the absence of prior experience and insufficient development of the touch organs. Growing in experience, the child's experiences of taste, shade and sound, as well as contact or stress are correlated to specific concrete devices. Gradually, the child begins to recognize distinctions. He is able to distinguish between things and is aware of the meanings. On one side, he can observe minute changes in quantity and the members of the family. On the other hand, he organizes his knowledge into new family members or "gestalts," in keeping with the Gestalt college of psychology. It also includes memories of the beyond enjoyment of the same object or an equivalent item. Beyond reports that can help in the growth of both personal and academic sets are crucial to faith. The child is able to perceive these things swiftly and quickly, and are connected to his interests as well as his intellectual units. The child's perceptions are determined by his desires and requirements. In a test, two groups of children, one bad group and the other, a wealth business were required to be able to see clearly and decide the sizes of the different coins presented to them. The poor group overestimated the size of the coins much more than the rich group due the fact that to the poor group, the money was significant in cost and usage.

Since the human woman gets older and is entering the early years of maturity, various aspects that impact his perception will be his beliefs, his opinions and values of the culture. The perceptions and feelings can be classified into eight types.

They are the olfactory, gustatory, tactual natural, kinesthetic body equilibrium, auditory and visible. They are called that because of the organ involved , which is the tongue, the skin and the nostril. The muscles, belly semi-circular canals ears and the focus.

Concept Formation

A term is generalized, meaning that it is connected to an object. It's not the product of our perceptions. For instance, 'horse", "house" or 'table' and 'guy' all are all concepts. We look at a variety of tables, horses or homes look at their most common characteristics and traits, and their relationships and then reach a generalized view. When we say horse, it's not the horse we saw; it is for all kinds of horses. This is how we arrive at notions of individuals, factors and characteristics, due to our sense of perception, our ability to analyze most common traits, and to relate the different traits way, and to abstract and generalize. "Residence", "Table" and 'cap' are the norms of things. Father's mother's name, 'trainer are the humane principles and honesty is a principle of ideas and traits. The development and acquisition of concepts is an amazing improvement in the mental development of children. It involves discrimination as well as generalization. The child's perception of the world are raised with pleasure, along with his ability to comprehend the relationships between different situations. While the concepts multiply in number along with a heightened levels of enjoyment and diversity these ideas, but they also become more affluent and fuller. The concepts of December could have an impact in the event that the child has lived this at Punjab, Delhi, Mumbai and Kolkata. It's because of this , that the modern curriculum offers the aid of travel or tours and trips to tourist destinations to make their experience more enriching and complete. These interactions and studies are sure to add more meaning and depth to the ideas that are formulated. The most efficient element that can contribute to the depth of knowledge of the old. As kids grow older and become more knowledgeable, they're able to study additional magazines, books, and seek out answers from humans. In this way, they expand their concepts of human beings, issues and ideas.

The ideas formed by young children, especially in the beginning stages are difficult to grasp due to three main reasons:

A lot of children's ideas are distinct from those of adults, and therefore the adult might not be aware of the meanings of these children's concepts. A child's definition of "doggie could also mean any small animal, whereas to an adult the meaning of "canine is specific. The child's expectations are generally board and well-known, not specific.

The standards of the child aren't developed correctly enough for your child to be able to convey them in terms that are understandable to the person.

A lot of children's standards are not "verbalized" as a due to the limited vocabulary.

The concepts of children's spatial relationships of distance and intensity, are hazy and insufficient at the beginning. This is the reason for much of the insecurity among younger children who make confusion about the relationship between distance and peak language development. The knowledge of phrases such as to, within, beneath over as well as down and up, which helps them recognize spatial connections. The growth of the concept of time involves proximity, beginning in relation to desire satisfactions and the habitual. They are aware of what the words is happening in the morning, at night and at night. refer to in terms of eating and eating, as well as sleeping. When they reach 5 years of age, children could be able to discern between the past, present and future. The way we measure time, they will be able to discern just with the help of around ten. The instructors of arithmetic must comprehend the data that might result from investigations. The notions of quantity and number are introduced at mind of children through the experiences they have in the family home that give children the concepts of 'much less' or 'more in the sense of being heavier or being 'mild'. According to Piaget children learn concepts that are diverse before they are not able to counting. They have a head start over the weight concepts. If the school and home give concrete and precise reports using diverse materials, these ideas can be quickly and naturally. Medical theories that involve subject causal relationships expand as kids are provided with a variety of problems and give explanations for or respond to questions. The concepts that are the basis of ability in inductive and deductive reasoning are developed with the passage of time. Self concepts and the social concepts of inter public relations significantly influence the child's behavior and questions and is an essential element in the development of the intellect of children. Beginning with the idea of self is to begin with the most basic physical identity. As time passes, the child begins to distinguish himself from the other. The child's social skills are boosted by the nature of the inter-personal relationships at home, through the use of his critiques of people in the neighborhood, at the playground as well as through other sports for social interaction. In addition, the child acquires notions of beauty, or aesthetics through his interactions with his books, readings, institutions, values of culture and his experience of coloration as well as form and voice i.e. the environmental effects. If a child is in filthy, boring and uncolored surroundings, there is an opportunity for him to develop false notions of the beauty of the form, color or sound. Education and training and models within the home can play an important role in commitment to the essence of these ideas.

Chapter 11: The Function Of Communication

Being able to communicate effectively with your child is a sign that you can be able to recognize their needs and requirements and respond to their needs by responding appropriately. The process begins from the time of infancy. It's not a new concept for parents to understand and acknowledge these requests at the time of the baby's birth. Babies cry and scream along and give a variety of cues to parents to meet their various needs, ranging from sleep or hunger to being uncomfortable or needing for a hug. Parents are generally skilled at recognizing these signals and reacting in a timely manner. Even before a child is able to speak in the first place, they communicate using signals. Cues such as pointing at the object of their choice when they are in need of something, such as for instance, a juice bottle or raising the hands of children when they require to be held are normal for children who are not yet able to speak. It is crucial that the parent or caregiver recognizes these signals and reacts in a manner that is appropriate.

Utilizing Appropriate Nomenclature

It is essential that children and parents adhere to using appropriate names for everyday used objects. A habit of using appropriate names for things that are commonly used will go a long way in making sure that your child can learn these items quickly and results in quicker communication. Making sure that you use the correct name for items that are used every day can help children to master quickly and utilize them in a proper manner.

Do not talk to babies. Talk

The child may not recognize the pronunciation of a specific word and could be able to call it their own version that may be a sound similar to the one you are using or a mixture of letters with similar sounds. For instance, a kid who would like to say 'juice but prefers to say "ja-ju.' This is perfectly fine and, although the child will begin to learn how to say juice in time but you can help them improve their learning speed by saying "juice" yourself, and not substituting 'ja-ju' for juice by yourself. When parents utilize baby talk in order in order to communicate with their child, it slows the process of learning for the child. Always use appropriate names for objects and also encourage your child to master this method of learning.

Be respectful of your child

Be sure to respect your child from early in the process. Even if they're still in their early years and are unable to speak and communicate in words Make it a priority to make them feel important when it comes to interactions. Include as often as you can.

If, for instance, you feed the child you might incorporate them into the meal with a question like, "Would you like to hold this spoon while mommy feeds you?"

If you're bathing your child and you are reciting rhymes while bathing as a play for bath time or activity, you can ask your child to name the rhyme they'd like to sing and then sing it together. The idea is to make your child feel loved, valued and valued. We want them and be able to believe that their thoughts and choices are important to us, and that we are willing to listen to their opinions. It is crucial to start to teach this belief at an early age. The feeling of being valued and appreciated is a significant factor in building confidence in children as early as.

Expression of Emotions

Being able to communicate their emotions effectively is essential to communicating effectively. To do this it is necessary for them to have our guidance and love to help them understand what they feel. Parents can assist their child with this by helping them identify the emotion they feel.

If, for instance, you see your child sat in a quiet spot after having said goodbye to their parents then you can say something such as, "I understand you must be sad since grandma went away for her vacation. Do you miss her already? It's okay to feel sad." Perhaps something like, "You are pounding the table, it's because you're angered."

The purpose of this method is to give the name to the situation they are through or feeling they feel. This can be extremely beneficial in the event that you want to help them learn how to behave or react in the event of experiencing similar feelings at some point in the near future.

For instance, you want to remind your child to focus on brighter or positive things whenever they're sad. To do this, they must be aware of what sadness is all about in its first instance. For instance, if their grandmother has gone on a trip, you'd like to help them see the bright side by saying, "You can make a welcome card for her when she returns." When your child is upset and you are frustrated, you could suggest, "Take a deep breath three times when you're angered." When your child can connect the word that describes the emotion to the feelings they felt the moment they experienced it can they take your advice and put it into action.

Naming emotions is essential when you are trying to teach your child what emotions are acceptable to express and which are best under control.

Positive Talk

Another key element to effective communication with children, particularly during the toddler years is to employ positive language. It is the case when your words are based on what your child is able or should do, in lieu of things they should, shouldn't do, shouldn't or shouldn't do.

Avoiding Negatives

Develop a habit of engage your child in positive words. If you are aware that the words you're going to say could be negation or denials of any kind, you can use an alternative positive in place of it. A simple "no" is more difficult for toddlers to think about than a positive alternative. Think about the following dialogue between two parents and a toddler:

Child: Could I go on a trip to the parks today?

Parent Not today, but not tomorrow.

Child: Why don't you go today? I'd like to go to the bathroom now! I am bored.

Parent: I've told you that you should not do it today. Play with your toys today.

The situation could quickly turn into a rage or even a complete meltdown. You can now see the same dialog with the negatives removed.

Child: May I go on a trip to the parks today?

Parent: I think we'll visit the park on Monday.

Child: I'm bored right now!

Parent: What if we play together with your toys today and then we visit the park on Monday?

It is evident that the child isn't asking "Why why not now?" in the second scenario , because the parent isn't saying, "Not today." Instead, they chose an alternative that is positive. Additionally, it is important to observe that the parent is involving the child in the process of confirming their decision-making process and activities, as well as offering the opportunity to interact with their child rather than the child. This is a crucial aspect to take note of.

Utilizing a 'no' often in response to your child's needs and requests can make the child into a bitter person from within. It creates the feeling of being rejected every time you are confronted with an unintentionally no. If the same story is conveyed in an alternative that is positive It doesn't cause the same impact and can be more encouraging and builds confidence for the child.

Reframing

Importantly, you must stay clear of constant negative messages. If a child is accustomed to hearing phrases like"don't do that or that regularly on a daily basis, it will cause resentment in the child's mind towards the parent. That's not the kind of thing a parent would wish for. Take a look at the following scenario to get a better understanding of the situation.

When your kid is running your home or lying onto the sofa, you're likely to tell them something along the lines of "don't jump" as well as "don't leap." Instead you can change the sentence to avoid the negative, and instead make it something like "We must walk around the home. It is okay to run on the lawn or in the playground," and "We jump on the ground and then sit on the couch."

It is possible to include some cautionary words in relation to the values that you adhere to at home, or their safety which could be in danger in the event of their conduct. However, you should never start your instructions or suggestions with the word "negative. Do not use the phrase "don't" in these instances.

By doing this, your child won't be deprived or be denied basic pleasures on a regular basis.

Practical Strategies to Improve Communication

There are a few practical ideas that you could apply and apply when you want to talk to your child easily and with efficacy. Keep these points in mind will allow you to speak in a way that your child will comprehend and, at the same time, appreciate what you're saying as the significance it holds. You'll be able connect with your child in a more effective way in this manner.

Maintaining Eye Level

Always try to engage with your children while you are on their level. Take a seat, in a knee-squat or bend your back to be on the same level as your child. Being at the same level with them is like getting them to feel confident before they say anything. This easy step can make you more approachable and easy to comprehend. Even if what you're talking about isn't orally intimidating but your rigid and uncompromising position can cause it to appear as if it is. It is an excellent idea to talk to children when they are on the similar level. In addition, if you are talking to them, and you're simply listening, being at their level indicates an interest on your part and your child will consequently be more likely to speak and be open to you in this manner.

Reiterate and affirm

If you child is trying to convey to you something, whether it's by using words, fully-framed sentences, or even gesticulations and cues It is always best to confirm their thoughts loud. Repeat the words to show them that you're listening and that you are prepared to listen to them out and comprehend their wishes or needs. This is particularly important for children younger than two years old who have only recently begun talking. It can help you comprehend them better even if you only have just a few phrases or gestures to follow. Repeating their thoughts and affirming them following them will give them an opportunity to recognize if what you've heard is what they've been trying to convey or to change their style to make it easier for you to understand.

For instance, "You are pointing at the teddy. Would you want you could play?" or

"I know you would like to eat ice cream, but let's get it together following dinner."

Narratives from the Parental Perspective

Narratives allow you to include your child in daily activities through talking with them about the tasks you're working on or telling them an account of your life or an amusing story of your youth. The idea is to engage them and get them to feel included. These short stories can create an environment that is comfortable around your child, and allow them to be comfortable in speaking to you in the same way whenever they're required to. This also helps them feel an impression of importance in knowing you consider they are important enough to be able to share these things with them. They are more likely to show appreciation in the future.

If, for instance, you're making an omelet, and your child is on a nearby table and you are cooking, speak to them about what you're doing with an easy narrative. Perhaps you can discuss an omelet to a story you had in your childhood. Making them feel included and appreciated is essential.

Chapter 12: Combat & Breathing

Choose Your Battles

Another way to stop temper tantrums right from the beginning is to learn to choose your fights. If you're constantly pointing fingers at your child in an effort to get them to perform exactly what you would like them to do, when you'd like you to make them do it what is the likelihood that you will be able to have constructive interactions? You'll constantly be criticizing your child and pointing out that every single thing that they do is wrong, and this could be devastating for toddlers. What you do is to encourage the child that whatever they do is problematic. You will point out that your child is always doing wrong, and, as a result you'll feel that your interactions with him are negative.

Of course, it isn't something you want to establish. If your child is conditioned to believe that interactions with you will turn out be negative, your child won't be inclined to interact with you in any way. You would like your interaction with them to be positive. To do this, you'll have to choose your battles carefully. If you choose your battles together with your kid, you will learn to ensure that the relationships you share with them aren't only negative.

The process of picking your battles is about weighing whether an issue is worthy of being a focus. You must determine whether the fight you choose is one that needs you to fight for initially or if it's something that's unlikely to cause any harm or cause any problems if it occurs. You must decide which battle you pick is going to have enough impact to make it worth the effort.

In this instance, you'll be required to determine whether or not the mistake you're trying to fix has a significant impact on the issue. If it's not worth addressing or if the effort could be better used elsewhere, then you must do precisely this. If you can be sure that the energy you use is directed in the direction that will yield the greatest efficiency it is clear that you're doing to the highest level you can within the limitations that you're facing.

Imagine your child making stacks of blocks, and then knocking them down and laughing. You might have the strictest no-hitting or throwing policy, but this rule is mostly because you don't want to break anything and you don't wish to encourage any type of violence with your kid and the other. It is important to determine and decide if your child is building blocks and pushing them to the ground is worth creating an uproar over. Do you really wish to make the situation a major issue even though nobody is injured and nothing is damaged?

Consider that scenario as your child randomly walking across and knocking down a neighbor's block tower. The difference between the two is that one is actually engaging in destruction and acting rudely to other people. When your child is playing with around other people's buildings, they might be angry or frustrated by some issue, or they might be convinced that kicking the blocks is fun. Are both of these scenarios require the same level of intervention?

If you are picking your battles, you're trying to make some kind of sense from the actions you're taking as well as the actions of your child and the best way to combine it all to ensure that you're not being too harsh with your child however, you should not be too lenient. It's a fine line to keep in keep in mind. In this instance, you have to decide where you'd like to draw the line in the middle of the sand.

In general it is possible to think of certain situations that are likely to need intervention, and other situations that may need intervention, and those that are totally acceptable for you. This is your method of determining what is best for your family and you and will differ from person to. For instance, some people don't create a food fight. They believe it is an issue the child can determine by themselves and allow the child to decide for themselves. They let their child decide if they are going to eat something, and should their child take an ounce of food and immediately declares that they don't like the food, their parents won't be too concerned. They let their children make these kinds of choices on their own to avoid fights that could otherwise happen and cause issues for all affected. There's no need to make your child be a certain way of living when they're not harming anyone, damaging things, or doing anything which is risky.

When looking to decide whether this is a fight you'd like to take on it is a good idea to consider thinking over the questions below, and then discussing the answers. These questions will assist you in determining whether this isactually something worthy of turning into a fight or to leave out.

Is it really worth the effort, energy and effort you have to argue over?

*Is my motivation to fight a result of my own anger or is it a genuine desire to change my behavior?

*What will be the best for the peace of this family today?

*Is this an isolated incident that doesn't happen often or is it a pattern that needs to be challenged to fix it?

Can I handle this in a manner that doesn't cause additional anger?

Ask your child what you can do to handle this circumstance?

Breathing Exercises

If your child is bursting into a screaming tantrum You may realize that you're determined to end it immediately. It is possible that you could get your child to calm down if you let them in or put your child in time out, you'll remove the entire issue. You can try whatever is in your mind with the hope to stop the rage before it escalates. Many think that calming a child's temper is almost impossible or they believe that their children are being difficult to control But you can assist your child in recognizing the cause, how the behavior is problematic at all and then how to end the behaviour completely. The solution is simple--all you have to do is to use breathing.

If you're emotionally tense, what can you do to to calm down, gain control and return to normal? A majority of people engage in deep breathing exercises. It is natural to do this. When you take a large deep breath, you alter the chest's pressure. The result is your heart rate needing to change to adjust this, due to the vagus nerve triggering. The vagus nerve, which controls your heart as well as your blood circulation, is responsible for relaxation and calm down. And when you take deep, long breaths, you are encouraging the body's muscles to ease. You can stop and unwind when you take the big, deep breaths and by doing so, you aid in helping you relax.

Even toddlers can learn to do this too. You might not be able to direct your child to take a deep air, but could help them with different strategies and techniques. You can basically help your child take deep, long breaths by playing with them and when they do this it will help them relax. It is a good idea to encourage this and then you can talk to your child the ways it can help them settle down easily. If you follow this method you'll discover that you can assist your child calm down.

As time passes Your children will learn to to soothe themselves and also. They begin to regulate themselves as they begin to connect deep breathing exercises to ways they can be calm. They do this to help themselves relax and can assist them in preventing yourself from throwing a fit too. They will be taught how to stop the tantrums by themselves, which will allow them to to regulate themselves.

Let's quickly look at three possible ways to prompt your child to take a deep breath and breathe deep to help them to relax. Remember that in order for these exercises to be successful over the long term it is important to make sure that they start by putting your child into a calmer and more peaceful state. This will allow for a variety of practice to ensure that your child understands what is expected. If you practice this regularly it will be evident that your child is in a position to perform these exercises easily whenever they are important.

Candles and flowers A method that children love to play with when they are struggling to breathe is by making use of fantasy and visualization. This can be done by inviting your child to smell the flower, while blowing out candles can be made to look like it is held. By doing this, you will encourage your child to slow down and breathe in order to allow them to truly begin to relax. To make the most impact, lead your child to sniff the flower of the scent that you know that your child is fond of, and then ask the child that they should blow on a huge birthday cake candle you hold. This will encourage the child to have a large, deep smell and a large and large blow.

"Belly breathing." This technique will also work in the same manner. You are inducing children to inhale through their stomach instead of through the chest, which people do when stressed. The only thing you need to do is ask your child to lay on his or their back, and put an animal toy or stone on the stomachs of their children. Then, ask your child to take a deep breath and observe the animal moving upwards and downwards when they do. This will not only help your child breathe but can also help your child become more engaged. Your child has become more engaged with playing with the toys and taken deep breaths to relax.

Playing with the feathers could play with feathers that you've discovered poking out of pillows made of down and coats. Or purchase feathers for crafting at the shop. If you use this method, you could invite your child to blow feathers in the air. They can throw the feather in the air, and then blow it around to make it move around. This gives you the added benefit of encouraging to take all kinds of large deep breaths, while making sure your child is not entertained by something exciting. It is possible to take this to the next level by having many varieties of different sizes and shapes. You and your child could play a game to see which take longer to complete than other.

Chapter 13: Difficult Toddlers

Common struggles that Toddlers can face
Children aren't able to grasp the reasoning behind waiting, and the reasoning of having everything. They don't know anything or nothing about self-control, and in the simplest terms, they might be having a difficult to balance their needs with the services you provide as caregiver or parent. Toddlers can be challenging and they may be fun to. Here are four typical situations your child might be having trouble with:

1. He does not say no when he says"yes. This happens when you're serving him his favorite food.

2. He gets angry whenever you are unable to comprehend his meaning.

3. He isn't looking for a substitute. Blue pajamas or any other even though they might not be cleaned or after he has offered to him the one in purple.

4. He is agitated when he gets angry. Gets angry and throws everything away.

The above listed actions are only the actions toddlers use to control their emotions, as they are not yet familiar with everything. They lack control over what they are able to control and how to control it. As young children, and they soon find that they possess vocal abilities and that's when their crying, screaming and screaming increase. They may also play around with different noises to determine how they sound , and also the reactions of adults to the noise. They can be impulsive and engage in the activity without thinking about it. It is essential to be aware that there is an individuality for each child. They respond differently to various circumstances; you can even put the child's name on them. Most of the time, you can begin with names that are funny, such as Daredevil, bubbly, determined and obstinate at times, cautious, adventurous, etc. It could be fascinating to know that a certain toddler behavior is actually developmentalally correct They could be aggressive and bossy, or sassy, or indecisive, but they are simply a part of what your child requires-independence.

Troublesome behaviors and their practical Solutions

Biting, Aggression, Hitting and Aggression

The tendency to be aggressive is common among toddlers. Don't be surprised if I've said it before. In this article, I will give you practical suggestions regarding what you should do when you meet an child who is aggressive.

Make sure to keep your cool: Keeping your cool will show how calm you are. Do not yell at your child when he/she's acting out. If you say to your child that she's wrong and you do this, you're just making her angry.

Please be specific about your boundaries The response you give to your toddler's aggressive behavior must be quick. Be sure that he/she is taken removed from the area for a short time-out. Perhaps just a few minutes will allow the child to calm down. Then, you reconnect to the child once he/she has realized the implications of the response.

*Promote good behavior: I've previously mentioned this behavior, and I would be willing to repeat it over and over again. You should give praise for good behavior right away you notice it. It is not a good idea to pay attention to your child only when he is acting out and then catch him doing something great and give him praise for it. The offer to push the swing or play with him should be an incentive to reward good behaviour.

Provide logical consequences If your child begins throwing Lego toys on other kids as they are playing, remove the child away right away and observe others playing. While doing this, tell your child that he or she can come back when they are eager to have fun, without harming other children. Don't be a lecturer or think like the toddler. It's impossible to argue with them right now since they don't fully comprehend the implications for their choices.

*Be consistent with your discipline Children are fond of repetition and as a result little bits of information are left where they are kept. Be sure to respond to every episode of aggression in the same way until you are predictable. This creates a pattern your child can recognize and strives to avoid. It will eventually become part of the child's consciousness.

Alternatives to be taught explain to the child in a short manner about the implications of their previous move. It is normal to have anger but it's not acceptable to express these feelings by hitting, punching or biting. It is important to apologize when he has yelled at anyone for any reason. The apology must be genuine even though it appears insincere to you. The lessons will be absorbed.

Keep your toddler active: If you suspect that your child is an active and energy one, make sure she has ample time to play unstructured, ensure that they are outdoors at least. This allows him time to burn off the excess energy.

Watch it If it's screen time as a parent, you should be attentive to what you child has been watching. Some cartoons are not designed for young children. Be wary of the online games and other forms of media that are specifically designed for children. Numerous studies have shown that excessive screen time can lead to negative behavior of children and can cause a lot of problems as they develop. It is important to know that American Academy of Pediatrics advises against using screens for TV or other devices that includes computers, phones and tablets until they are at the age of 18 months. Even when your child is months old, it is best to restrict his screen time to no more than one hour per day. Select what she is watching, and make sure it is quality, appropriate for her age. A war-themed film that has many combat scenes would not be suitable for a child who is aggressive. It could only raise the level of aggression to something violent or even extreme.

If you are in need of assistance: Talk to an experienced child physician If you are concerned that your child's behavior is excessive. However, this should only be the case if you've noticed any or all of these characteristics:

Your child has no problem finding it easy to slash at adults.

He or she loves making others children angry or scared.

They are in a state of rage for more than few weeks after having attempted everything you can.

Interrupting

There is nothing more frustrating as a child who seems to will interrupt you whenever you chat with your friend. Toddlers aren't really interrupted by verbal utterances all the time, however their actions. It is because they are always seeking to be noticed by their parents. And they could be jealous when someone else, whether a parent or a friend gets all the attention. In this regard it's your fault. The following are options:

Pick the ideal location for your meeting. An area that your children can enjoy themselves while you converse with your adult. A park with Sandboxes is a nice thing.

Find a babysitter. This can be extremely helpful and let you keep your full concentration or focus throughout the meeting. You can rest assured you are safe in the hands of a professional.

*Teach your children polite behavior. One way to teach your children is to read them some books , such as The Berenstain Bears Forget Their Manners written from Stan as well as Jan Berenstain or The Bad Good Manners Book written by Babette Cole's aliki's Manners And What Do you say Dear? by Sesyle Joslin. Any good-manners book that you can get your fingertips on. It is a good book to read to your children every day.

*Schedule your phone calls. You don't want your child to interrupt your call while you're making a phone call, so you should make the necessary arrangements.

False

First, what is the reason children lie? They have a vivid imagination, and are very insensitive. They may be suffering from what is known as angel syndrome. The child who believes the parents believe that he is able to do wrong will be prone to commit wrongdoing with intent. If asked, the word "liar" occurs to the mind. Children lie, and it's natural for them to lie. How do you stop this?

*Always encourage truth-telling. Don't be angry at your child if they speak the truth, but instead be content. Teach your child that honesty is rewarded.

You should not be accusing your child without cause. Your words, comments, and actions will help your child and not degrade him.

Do not burden your child by imposing too many demands on them. They won't be able to comprehend. They're toddlers, children not adults. Don't expect too much of them.

* Build your confidence. Make sure your child knows that you trust him/her her, and do not break the trust.

Pulling Hair

In the beginning the basics, pulling hair and biting, pinching hitting, etc. are all ways that your child displays his emotions or exerts control over what appears to be his current surroundings (his body). Roberts is a professor of psychotherapy of Idaho State University in Pocatello says that "a child may be pulling hair to make unpleasant things disappear." Whatever the reason, it is important to be aware of the following actions when this happens:

Let them be aware that this won't work. Proving convincingly that an aggressive act will result in nothing is the best way to stop the urge to be aggressive. Do not ignore it, prove the absurdity of pulling hair, and make sure that he comprehends that.

Stop the behavior as soon it begins. If you spot him holding an oversized amount of hair Stop him immediately. Keep his hands in place as you repeat this phrase "we do not pull our hair. The pain of pulling hair is too much."

Make sure you provide a thorough explanation however, make sure that it is concise. The first step is to ask your child or friend "what was it that you did which was not right?" after the reply then you take the opportunity to inform that pulling your hair is only damaging himself and other people.

*You are not responsible for the same crime. Don't pull the hair of your child If you don't wish them to pull their hair too.

Running Away

A toddler running away could be quite funny. Really? What are they thinking they're going? You must be cautious when it occurs outdoors, particularly on the sidewalk. What is the reason they are running? Like any other behavior shown by a toddler the reason for running away is an increase in autonomy and also the realization that he's got legs which can run. Patricia Shimm, director of the Barnard College Center for Toddler Development in New York and co-author of Parenting Your Toddler says "toddlers enjoy the sensation of running around and being independent. around. You can inspire them to do it as long as you manage where they go." There is no way to stop it; you only have control over it:

Stay close to them and it is safe for you to watch ahead when they're moving.

Show him the areas where he can run, and also where he shouldn't. Allow him to explore safe zones
• Engage your child.

Chapter 14: Dealing with Troublesome Toddlers

We know that toddlers aren't always easy, which is where the need for training their minds comes into. Do not assume that they'll understand when they're grown up, however. it might be difficult to stop once they're mature. They're toddlers and they're not stupid and they are aware of the distinction between right and wrong. As you read the beginning, we are at the heart of this book . I'd suggest that you go through this book in a non-biased manner. What I am saying here might not be in line with your thought process, however an open mind can encourage you to consider the issue from various perspectives.

Four common struggles that toddlers may Be Having

To begin, it is important to know why toddlers can be challenging. For the first moment, they're recognizing that they are distinct individuals from their caregivers and parents. The initial impression of a baby is that they are part of the family however once they get to the stage of toddlerhood, they realize this isn't the case. It also means that they begin to push themselves and communicate their opinions and dislikes, as well as striving to be independent. They also try to learn the skills of language that will enable them to express their ideas, desires or requirements.

In addition, toddlers do not comprehend the concept of waiting or the rationale for having everything. They know nothing about self-control. In an e-book, he/she might be having a difficult in balancing their needs and the things you offer as the parent or caregiver. Toddlers can be challenging and can be fun to. Here are four typical situations your child may be having trouble with:

He doesn't say"no" when he is saying yes. This happens when you're serving him his favorite food.

He can be irritable if you don't understand his language.

He's not interested in any other. Blue pajamas or the other, despite the fact that they're not washable or even after giving to him the one in purple.

He screams when he is angry. Gets angry and throws everything away.

The above listed actions are just a few of the behaviors toddlers use to control their emotions, as they are still new to nearly everything. They lack control over what is controlling them and how they manage it. When they are young children, and they soon find that they possess vocal abilities and that's when their crying, screaming and yelling increase. They might also play around with different sounds to test what they sound like and the reactions of adults to these sounds. They can be impulsive and engage in the activity without any thought. It is essential to be aware that there is certain characteristics in every child. They respond differently to various circumstances, and you can even put the child's name on their tag. Most often, they will be greeted with some fun names such as bold, daredevil and obstinate or cautious. It could be fascinating to know that a certain toddler behavior is actually develop mentally correct They could be aggressive as well as bossy, sassy and indecisive, but they are simply a an expression of what a child is looking for- independence.

Eleven difficult behavior types and their practical Solutions

However, certain bad behavior are typical among toddlers. Here are the top 11 challenging behavior patterns and their solutions:

Biting and aggressively hitting
Interrupting
Illusory
Hair pulling
The runaway
Screaming
Tattling
Teasing
Disrupting the peace
Dispersing objects
Whining
Biting, Hitting, and Aggression

It is normal to see aggressive behavior in toddlers, so don't be shocked if I've already said that. In this article, I will give you practical suggestions regarding what you should do when you encounter an child who is aggressive.

Keep your cool: Keeping your cool shows how calm you are. Don't shout at your child when they are in a rage mode. If you are telling your child she's wrong it is just getting her angry.

Be clear about your boundaries What you do with your toddler's aggressive behavior must be quick. Make sure that the child is taken removed from the scene for a short time-out. Perhaps a few minutes is enough to allow them to relax. Then, you reconnect to the child once they have been able to comprehend the consequences of the response.

Encourage good behavior: I've discussed this particular behavior before and will continue to say this again. You should praise good behavior as soon as when you observe it. It is not a good idea to be able to give your child praise only when he is acting out and then catch him doing something great and praise him for it. A suggestion to push his swing or to play together be an incentive for good behavior.

Give logical consequences If your child begins throwing Lego toys at children as they are playing, you should take your child away immediately and observe others playing. While doing this, tell your child that he/she is able to return when they are willing to play without hurting others. Don't be a lecturer or think like the toddler. It's impossible to argue with them right now since they aren't aware of the implications that their behavior has.

Be consistent in your discipline children love rote learning and, as a result there are bits of information in their storage. You must respond to each incident of aggression in the same manner and you will become predictable. This will create a pattern children recognize and try to avoid. It will eventually become part of the child's consciousness.

Alternatives to be taught: Inform him or her in brief terms the consequences of his their last behavior. It is normal to feel anger, but it's not appropriate to display that anger by hitting, kicking or biting. You should make an apology after slamming an individual for whatever reason. An apology must be sincere , even though it might appear unsincere to you. In this way, the lessons will be absorbed.

Make sure your toddler is active If you observe that your child is an active and energy one, make sure she has lots of free time. ensure that they are outdoors at least. This allows him time to use up all of his energy.

Be attentive Watch it: When it comes to screen time as a parent, you must be attentive to what you child has been watching. There are many cartoons that aren't designed for youngsters. Be aware of digital games and other forms of media that are intended for children. A number of studies show that prolonged screen time is a factor in the poor behavior of children and can cause a lot of problems as they get older. It might be interesting to know that the American Academy of Pediatrics advises against using screens for TV or other devices such as computers, phones and tablets until your child is at minimum 18 months old. Even when your child is months old, it is best to limit the amount of time he spends on screens to no more than one hour per day. Make sure she chooses what she's watching and select the best quality, age-appropriate content. A war-themed film that has many combat scenes isn't suitable for a child who is aggressive. It could only raise the intensity of his aggression to something violent or even extreme.

Seek help if you require assistance: Contact an experienced child physician when you feel that your child's behavior is getting too much. However, this should only be the case if you've observed any or all of these signs:

Your child is able to slash at adults.

Conclusion

Toddler discipline isn't an unfavourable concept that is filled with strategies to teach your child to manage using the left brain and to work swiftly to prevent the right-emotional brain from taking over. The strategies you learned were twenty beginning with the basics of child development and behavior of parents through practical guidance and examples to aid you in handling specific circumstances.

Deciding when it is appropriate to discipline your kid is extremely crucial, and it's important to be sure to thoroughly examine your child prior to making a decision to punish them. Are they simply doing something out of boredom are there more fundamental motivation behind the things they do?

Here are some occasions when you should correct your child's behavior:

If their actions place them in danger . For instance, if your child is rushing to the stove, and you warn them to stay away do it, they will instinctively continue to do it. This could lead them to be injuredand could put them at risk. The goal of discipline is to assist children understand the distinction between right and wrong actions. You should make sure you discipline the child is continuing to engage in things that could put them at risk.

When their actions place people in danger - For example, if you child has been covering their face by a pillow, playing games with their big sister and their long locks, or performing anything else that puts others in danger, then this is another reason to penalize them. You must first clarify to your child why their behavior is not right, however once they've been warned, you must follow-up with the sanction to assist to ensure that they don't hurt others.

If their actions harm anyone or something. For instance, if they're running around your house, they may smash something, break it, them or hit you. It may cause you to fall the infant. If their actions are likely to have the potential of harming the person or thing they are causing harm it is essential to ensure that you adhere to any promise of discipline to show them how crucial it is.

When they intentionally take a different path than the instruction you provide - If you say to your child, "Don't do this" and they do the opposite this is a clear violation and they must be taught to become more disciplined. It is crucial to help them understand that obedience is crucial, as it can save their life or even prevent the possibility of serious injury to them and others.

It is crucial to keep discipline to the times that are crucial and do not just spend your time disciplining or kicking your child for acting out. You must ensure that the actions are severe enough to require discipline. This will enable you avoid spending the entire time shaming your child.

Now you have the tools available to become the kind of parent that your child needs. You are able to begin implementing the strategies to deal with the different situations that come up to ensure that you're raising a content healthy and healthy toddler with confidence, responsibility respect, and curiosity.

Be aware of the golden rules that are to be attentive, repeat the steps, suggest an answer, and then rectify the issue in the long haul instead of thinking that one lesson will work. Your child is wonderful and deserves to be respected in all that you do even in instances when you have to make use of kind-ignoring in order to change the brain to be more peaceful that is listening to you just in the same way you pay attention to your toddler.

You are in the position to mold your child's personality or even harm your child. Through the content and methods, you have to take the initiative to apply what you've learned to your advantage and even employ reverse-psychology to help keep your child entertained and engaged in learning. You may want to instill ethics, values of honor, ethical methods, or confidence, there are tools included in this book to refer to whenever you need.

Take advantage of this stage in your toddler's world, when everything and anything is exciting, thrilling and exciting. As your child gets older into a teenager, they'll settle down, and stop getting involved in things, but they will require your love and attention. Respect and love are the two things you must never keep from your child, even when they are when your child is in the midst of an upset.

www.ingramcontent.com/pod-product-compliance
Lightning Source LLC
Chambersburg PA
CBHW071839080526
44589CB00012B/1055